By the same author:

Britain on the Couch

They F*** You Up

Affluenza

The Selfish Capitalist

Contented Dementia

How Not To F*** Them Up

Love Bombing

Office Politics

How to Develop Emotional Health

Oliver James

MACMILLAN

First published 2014 by Macmillan
an imprint of Pan Macmillan, a division of
Macmillan Publishers Limited

Pan Macmillan
20 New Wharf Road, London N1 9RR
Basingstoke and Oxford
Associated companies throughout the world
www.panmacmillan.com

ISBN 978-0-230-77171-0

9 8 7 6 5 4 3 2 1

A CIP catalogue record for this book is
available from the British Library.

Cover design by Marcia Mihotich
Typeset by seagulls.net
Printed and bound by CPI Group (UK) Ltd,
Croydon, CR0 4YY

Visit **www.panmacmillan.com** to
read more about all our books and to
buy them. You will also find features,
author interviews and news of any
author events, and you can sign up for
e-newsletters so that you're always first
to hear about our new releases.

Contents

Introduction:
Are You Emotionally Healthy?

Emotional health is the sense that what is happening, is happening now. It is experiencing the world as first-hand, immediate, rather than only knowing what was experienced when you reflect upon it later. You are, as the sports commentators put it, 'in the zone'.

You feel real rather than false. You are comfortable in your skin: you do not wish you could be someone else, nor do you look down on others for not being like you. You know what you are thinking and feeling, even if sometimes that only means knowing that you don't know.

You have your own consistent ethical code which enables you to distinguish right from wrong. You are stoical in the face of adversity, realistic in your ideas and often seem to be wise in your judgements. You have the capacity for insight into your own actions. You can sometimes spot in advance when you are about to make a mistake and avoid it, or can see when you are reacting irrationally to a situation and correct yourself – so having crashed the car, you do not do it again; you can notice that the lights have changed or a wall is approaching, and turn the steering wheel. This gives you that nectar of the soul, the capacity for choice, and therefore, for change. Such self-awareness is what sets us apart from other animals.

In your moment-to-moment dealings with other people, you are a good judge of what they are feeling and thinking. You are able to live in the place where self and others meet, without tyranny. You do not get either 'jammed on transmit' or 'jammed on receive'. You live without flooding or dominating others, nor are you flooded or dominated.

You are adaptable, but without losing yourself. When in social or professional situations which demand a measure of falsehood, you can put on a face to meet the faces that you meet without losing your sense of authenticity. Your real self is as close as possible to the one you are presenting to others, depending on what is feasible. For if a lie is necessary, you lie.

Your vivacity is striking, there is a liveliness you bring to any situation, but it is not frenetic and does not smack of 'keeping busy' to distract from bad feelings. You are spontaneous and always searching for the playful way to handle things, retaining a child-like sparkle, a conviction that life is to be enjoyed, not endured. You are not bogged down in needy, childish, greedy, game-playing manipulation.

You may suffer depressions, rages, phobias, all manner of problems, from time to time. You make mistakes. But because of your emotional health, you are able to live in the present and find the value in your existence, whatever is going on, and this makes you resilient.

When people leave your presence, they often feel better able to function, more vivacious and playful. Your emotional wellness rubs off on them. You are no martyr but you are widely regarded as a valuable contributor to your social and professional circles.

Have you ever met anyone like this? No, nor have I.

But this is what I mean by emotional health. None of us are emotionally healthy at all times, in all these ways. Most of us achieve it only in some of the respects outlined above, and only some of the time; very few manage this kind of emotional health in many of those respects and most of the time – perhaps 5 or 10 per cent of us. Helping you to edge closer to emotional health is the object of this book.

Who has emotional health?

Possessing emotional health has nothing to do with how intelligent or attractive or ambitious or rich you are. In fact, it is possible that high achievers are the least likely to be emotionally healthy, of any group. Many emotionally healthy people have relatively low-paid, low-status jobs and focus more on their home than their work lives.

Most of us are born emotionally healthy. A baby knows exactly who he or she is. Most toddlers know who they are and, when they feel safe, are spontaneously joyful. The play of small children offers a model to all adults. It is usually when children go to school, especially from ages seven to nine, that the challenges to emotional health arise most visibly. As the pressure to fit in and compare themselves with others builds, it becomes increasingly normal not to be emotionally healthy. Not until late middle age or old age, after a long period of being largely defeated by the challenges, does emotional health begin to return, if at all. As Oscar Wilde put it, 'To live is the rarest thing in the world. Most people exist, that is all.'

One way to look at it is as a kind of seven ages of emotional health, akin to Shakespeare's Seven Ages of Man, in which we start off healthy and only become that way again towards the end. This may be borne out by three massive surveys of mental illness in the

British population, according to which the group most likely to suffer from mental illness are those aged sixteen to twenty-four, with a steady decline in mental illness from then on, reaching the lowest levels in old age. Once you have passed early adulthood, your likelihood of being mentally healthy improves with each year.

What emotional health is not

But it is important to remember that emotional health is not defined by either mood or sanity. It is a different matter from mental health. An emotionally healthy person could be depressed or deluded, although this is probably rare.

Emotional health is defined by the positives described above, whereas mental health is largely defined negatively, by the absence of mental illnesses like anxiety, or more extreme problems like the mood swings of bipolar disorder. Nonetheless, it is interesting that when rare attempts are made to measure mental health (rather than mental illness) *positively*, it is found to be almost as rare as the emotional variety. An American psychologist called Robert Keyes did a thorough study of 3,000 people. Only 17 per cent of them were 'completely mentally healthy', defined as flourishing and without any signs of mental illness.

It is very abnormal for an adult in any developed nation to be completely emotionally healthy. Indeed, it may be rare in all urbanized, industrialized settings. At the risk of invoking idealized Noble Savages, it may only be the norm in pre-industrial settings – small villages or hunter-gatherer (itinerant) societies with no settled agriculture; it is certainly not so in our modern society.

Happiness is a fleeting state, the feeling of pleasure you gain from sex or a cigarette.

Nor should emotional health be conflated with ideas like 'life satisfaction' or 'well-being', nor with happiness. This latter is usually a fleeting state, the feeling of pleasure you gain from sex or a cigarette, or the satisfaction on hearing of a successful exam result. Beware of authors bearing gifts of happiness. It is psychological snake oil. In this author's opinion, we were not put on this earth to be happy, but it is plausible to suppose that we can be more emotionally healthy.

Nature versus nurture

A question may be forming in your mind: why do you and your siblings, or your offspring, vary in terms of emotional health? It is one of modern science's best-kept secrets that the answer is almost certainly little or nothing to do with genes.

For twelve years now, the Human Genome Project has been taking large groups of people who all share a specific problem, like depression or hyperactivity, and comparing their genes with an equivalent group without the problem. Very little genetic difference has been found. At most, so far, it explains only 5 to 10 per cent of almost all illnesses that have been studied. This even goes for rare and extreme problems, like schizophrenia (with symptoms like delusions or hallucinations). Scientists have been able to look at over a million genetic locations in each individual. Yet 90 to 95 per cent of the differences between different groups – schizophrenic versus non-schizophrenic, for instance – is not genetic. Since all the most plausible genetic loci have been scanned, it now seems very likely that this will be the final conclusion of the Human Genome Project. The implications are huge. The role of genes in emotional health is probably negligible, even nonexistent in many cases – just 5 to 10 per cent. It looks as if genes have been largely removed from the great Free Will versus Determinism debate. As you will see, a world of possibilities opens up.

In developed nations, emotional health is clearly linked to our life experience, and there are four main experiences that, individually or combined, lead to emotional health in adulthood. The first is being loved in the early years, and wisely nurtured subsequently. The second is receiving the right kind of supportive, loving assistance in the wake of childhood adversity, such as the loss of a parent, so that the person is able to convert the lead of such adversity into emotional gold. The third is to be prompted by a radical, severe shock in adulthood to undertake a complete rethink of life, resulting in a sudden appreciation of the gift of life itself. The last cause is profound spiritual or therapeutic experience.

If you have not had these experiences, despair ye not. By no means do I pretend that, simply by reading this book, you will ascend to a permanent and transcendent state of emotional health – in fact, as I have said, truly emotionally healthy people are very rare. However, with the right knowledge, everyone can become emotionally healthier; I can hold out that promise.

In this book I have summarized the key elements of emotional health under five headings:

1. Insightfulness: the ability to understand, by looking to the past, why you might think, feel and act a certain way.

2. Living in the present: the ability to have a strong sense of self, to own your own identity and live in the present instead of living 'as if' you are you, playing a role.

3. Fluid, two-way relationships: the ability to interact freely and comfortably, with a good sense of tact and an assertive manner, neither dominating nor passive.

4. Authenticity: the ability to live by values you identify with and believe in, rather than values you take on unthinkingly by default, often manifesting itself in your attitude to work and career.

5. Playfulness and vivacity: the ability to approach life with liveliness and joy.

With the help of case studies throughout, I shall show you how to achieve each of these elements, so that you can edge closer to emotional health; at the same time I will reveal some of the challenges represented by your infant and childhood experience that might be holding you back. If you meet these challenges, emotional health could happen to you.

Beware of authors bearing gifts of happiness. It is psychological snake oil.

1. Insightfulness

The smell of freshly cut grass reminds you of springtime as a small child, evoking images of your sweaty father ploughing up and down the lawn.

A song comes on the radio taking you straight back to the first time you met a lover.

As you slice the toast into strips for your child's dippy egg, you recall how negligent your mother was in distributing the butter equally across the bread, so that each soldier had some on it.

These are common kinds of 'conscious' memories: we know that our present experience is sometimes informed by the past. Less well known is the extent to which this is happening all the time, without our realizing it. At a fundamental level, how we were cared for in the early years is constantly affecting how we feel and react today, for better and worse. Having the insight to identify the early patterns that reduce emotional health, and building on the ones which amplify it, are the main routes to emotional health.

Sometimes, it can be just a matter of deleting bad habits learnt from our parents. Jim's dad tended to lecture people; Jim was the same, harming his relationships. Sarah's mum was chaotically disorganized; so was she, making it impossible for Sarah to be relaxed and positive, reducing her vivacity. For these individuals, just realizing that they did not have to be like their parents in these respects allowed them to reap a rich emotional harvest. Alas, our problems and opportunities can be much deeper than that, unconscious, in other words, and therefore less easily identified.

The actress Mia Farrow was the fifth of eight children. Speaking at the age of nineteen, she believed that this meant she had been starved of love and affection, yet over the next twenty years she became the mother of fourteen, and now claims that being in a large family is beneficial. She would seem to have lacked insight into herself, a component of emotional health so crucial for enabling change, and instead, appears to have repeated her own family history.

But if pathology can cascade down the generations, so can emotional health. Ian was a much-loved son, his mother greatly enjoying his playfulness when he was small and, subsequently, they shared a subtle sense of humour. Both mother and son had many problems, but their sense of the comic was rarely stifled. The jokes were not attempts to compensate for misery, not of the 'you have to laugh or you would cry' variety, they were done for fun. When Ian became a father, he developed a similar pattern with his son. They tend to foster this humorous playfulness in all situations, albeit there are other aspects of their relationship that are less emotionally healthy. Ian is working hard to identify these less-helpful patterns and develop others.

The positive features of relations with parents are much easier for us to think about than the negative. As tiny children, we depend completely on our parents for our physical survival, so the love of a baby or toddler for its carer is unconditional. That often endures into adulthood. We are tremendously protective of parents. Deep down, we fear that airing criticism of our parents will lead to our

The actress Mia Farrow was the fifth of eight children and she herself became the mother of fourteen.

being abandoned or rejected, and prefer to characterize ourselves as having had a happy childhood, whatever the reality. The most startling example I ever encountered was when I met the daughter of famous British serial killer Fred West. Despite having been repeatedly raped and brutalized, she was fierce in her defence of him.

In what follows, it is important that you understand that I am not trying to stir up trouble between you and your parents. I will not be encouraging you to become furiously reproachful or miserable about what went wrong. Rather, it is a case of understanding. If you can gain an accurate knowledge of how you were cared for as a child and develop insight into how it governs your present experience, it can transform who you are. The knowledge will ultimately improve your relationship with your parents, not poison it, and help create emotional health.

Before we go any further, there is a very important piece of information that needs reiterating: your emotional health is almost certainly not in the genes which you inherited. Health and illness both tend to run in families, and until now it was widely assumed that genes were the main reason. So if not them, then what?

Childhood

For several decades it has been increasingly clear that our early experience and subsequent childhood is critical in determining our emotional health in later life. At least twenty different studies suggest that the earlier we suffer maltreatment, the greater and more long-lasting the harm. For instance, among 800 children followed from birth to age nine, the ones who had suffered severe maltreatment before the age of three were more disturbed than those who had suffered it only between the ages three and five. The latter group in turn were more disturbed than children who had only suffered it aged five to nine.

The specific form of the maltreatment also predicted the type of later disturbance. For instance, children who were physically neglected had different outcomes from those who had been physically abused. Furthermore, the levels of cortisol, the 'fight–flight' hormone which is secreted in response to threat, were abnormally high if they had suffered maltreatment such as neglect, whereas cortisol levels were abnormally low if they had only suffered occasional physical abuse. Other studies suggest that, had these children's *brains* been tested, abnormalities in electrochemistry and structure would increase in severity according to how early the maltreatment occurred.

Our first six years play a critical role in shaping who we are as adults, physically and psychologically.

The tree of emotional health

Our emotional evolution is like climbing the branches of a tree. At each stage, depending on how we are cared for, we proceed along a different branch. If you think of the top of the tree as emotional health, the danger is that early deprivation or maltreatment traps us on a low branch. That sprouts new twigs which sprout still more, till we find ourselves at the end of a self-destructive branch – perhaps we are addicted to stimulation, a workaholic with the attention span of

Our emotional evolution is like climbing the branches of a tree.

a flea, who cannot sit still and is prone to gambling or casual sex or binge drinking.

Take Simon, now in his fifties, who had a successful banking career. His mother never managed to tune into him as a baby, so she could not recognize his signals – that he was hungry, or wanted a cuddle, or was tired. This left him permanently anxious, never sure if he was safe or whether his hunger would be satisfied, pretty much having to look after himself. As a toddler, it was no better. He was dumped abruptly with a succession of carers who had minimal knowledge of, or interest in, his specific wishes. By age three, he was a jumpy child who did not mix well with others. His father added to the problems by being increasingly enraged at Simon's behaviour, lashing out at him, sometimes using a shoe to beat him. The cruelty of these beatings amounted to abuse.

When Simon started school, he felt angry and isolated, making him unpopular. However, both his parents were highly intelligent and successful, and demonstrating his own intelligence and success became the only way he could get their attention. Simon quickly learnt to use his cleverness to do well at school. Whilst his teachers complained that he was badly behaved in and out of class, they were impressed by his marks on tests. He fell in with a few other pupils who were similarly angry or insecure. Some were the sort of children who get bullied, some were bullies – like Simon. As a group, on the whole, they were up to no good.

At this point, you can see that Simon had gone down a branch which was shared by other children like him and this only served to make his behaviour worse. But it is a myth that peers are a major influence on children. Our prior early childhoods determine which friends we make, and that in turn reinforces what we are like.

Simon's parents were forever being called in by the headmaster to hear of the latest atrocities – shoplifting, bullying, disobedience. Nothing anyone said made any difference, and as you can imagine, when he entered the teenage years, he and his gang were the first to be smoking, trying drugs, having sex. Nonetheless, he continued to use his cleverness to succeed in exams, so despite his delinquency, he proceeded to a top university. He had become an impatient young adult, always searching for the next distraction; to be still was his worst nightmare: he would immediately be assailed by a nameless fear, a sadness and an anger dating all the way back to the cot.

By the time he graduated from university he was already addicted to smoking or sniffing heroin. He had taken plenty of marijuana, cocaine and amphetamines, but from the first time he smoked heroin he instantly felt he had found a new home, somewhere he was safe. It took him to a calm, dreamy world. He could watch himself watching others, he even became nice to know, no longer a bully. Apart from a small coterie of fellow addicts, his social circle did not realize he was taking the drug. It did not much reduce his academic efficacy.

Having obtained a good degree, for a few years he did very little before taking a job in a merchant bank. He was witty, smart and, so long as he had taken heroin, personable. Whilst it was noticed that he could sometimes seem a bit frantic (during the gaps between drug use), that was normal in his world, a frenzied deal-making department of the bank. He was comfortable with the hectic atmosphere – it soaked up his unease and nerviness.

After various unhappy love affairs, he eventually married a woman who also was prone to drug-taking and they started a family. He was an affectionate, if erratic and tempestuous, father and husband. From time to time he would kick the drugs, but never for more than a year or two. In his forties he took heroin continuously but still succeeded in his career.

When Simon was fifty-two, the bank conducted a random drug test and, much to his managers' surprise, Simon was exposed. Forced to leave, he joked that he would have to start a new profession as a novelist: the title of his first book would be *High Finance* (sadly he never wrote it – he could have produced something very amusing).

Simon had some elements of emotional health, most notably his playfulness (often expressed in amusing wordplay), and from time to time a rich capacity to live in the present. But for the most part he inhabited the unreality of drugs and this meant that, in person, he was often unaware of what he or others were feeling and thinking, and this distorted his relationships. He also lacked insight into the roots of his own behaviour and, therefore, the capacity for change.

Although unusual in some of its details, Simon's story is no more representative a journey up the tree of emotional health than any other. Everyone's history illustrates certain fundamentals. Research has shown how, as a result of experiences we have in the womb and onwards, all of us develop unique patterns of brainwaves and levels of key chemicals in our nervous systems. These are primarily dictated by the kind of nurture we experience. They become the electrochemical thermostatic base levels to which our system returns, all other things being equal. Just as your house's central heating or air conditioning come on and off depending on the temperature, so our brains adjust the patterns of neuronal firing and chemical levels in response to the emotional warmth or coldness of the environment. Early experiences set our unique basal thermostatic levels and patterns.

Your emotional thermostat

Almost from the moment we are conceived, the growth of our brain and the chemicals in it are affected by the physical and emotional state of our mother. For example, if she is stressed during the last three months of the pregnancy, she secretes large quantities of cortisol, the 'fight–flight' hormone. These high levels are passed through the tube which connects the mother to the foetus. Years later, at age nine, her child will be twice as likely to be suffering from aggressiveness and attention deficit hyperactivity disorder (ADHD, a disorder defined by symptoms that include a short attention span and a tendency to rush about).

Even after you have taken into account how the child is cared for subsequently, on its own the high cortisol in the foetus puts the child at greater risk. But the high levels can also set off a chain of unfortunate consequences.

Such babies are liable to be born irritable or jumpy or floppy, potentially affecting how the mother reacts. If she is very responsive, the cortisol levels drop and the baby becomes routinely calm by the end of the first year of life. In Simon's case, his mother was not only stressed during the pregnancy, but because of her own history she was unable to respond to his difficultness when born. Since he was already jumpy, he was vulnerable. Her lack of responsiveness and subsequent care meant that he became a very twitchy, angry and sad 3-year-old. His father's abusive behaviour only served to make matters worse. By the time he was six and going to school, his electro-chemical thermostat was set at a baseline level that spelled trouble.

Whilst the accident of his parents' appreciation of intelligence fostered abilities which were to enable him to have successful educational and professional careers, that did not take away his fundamental sense of unease. He embarked along the branch of delinquency from a young age and proceeded eventually towards the leafy haze of the addictive shoots near the end of that branch.

As we shall see again over the course of this book, different aspects of what we are like are affected by care at different ages in our development. The first year establishes our deepest sense of who we are, the strength and solidity of our identity. Between six months and three years, the responsiveness of our parents and the consistency of the care we receive affects how emotionally secure we are in relationships. Between three and six, the way we are rewarded and punished, and the way our parents pass on their values to us (either coercing us to adopt them, or enabling us to feel we are *choosing* to adopt them) determines our basic levels of moti-vation and conscience, expressed in our careers. All of this means that, by age six, we are already hugely influenced by our upbringing (indeed, by age three, the differences in mental ability between the social classes have already been nurtured) and that affects what kind of friends we are drawn to, what sort of hobbies we take up, and our attitude to teachers and schooling. Soon we begin to be classified by our social world as 'bright' or 'lively' or 'moody', depending on our early childhood experiences. And these classifications quickly turn into self-fulfilling prophecies.

Of course, it is not all done and dusted at age six. What happens subsequently can radically affect which branches we move along, for good and ill. Severe abuse or a radically better kind of nurturing (as may happen if parents divorce and instead of an abusive father, a tender and loving stepfather appears) can dramatically alter the route taken. Alas, in most cases, that does not happen. All parents vary to some extent in how they react to their children at different stages – some prefer babies to toddlers, others only really enjoy over-threes, and this has variable results. But if you have benign parents early on, they tend to stay that way; likewise if your parents are the opposite. That is why it is so hard for us to clamber back along the low-hanging branches of addiction, emptiness or despair on which we are liable to become stranded, and return to the tree trunk in order to set off upwards. Our early years can send us in unfortunate directions, and in the absence of an alternative emotional map, we just cling on to the familiar.

The branching analogy shows why it is so hard for us to change, something that is crucial for emotional health. From birth onwards, our IQ and personality characteristics (like being shy or aggressive) usually do not much alter. By age thirty, our proneness to common emotional problems, like depression or anxiety, is well-established. If you have already suffered them by then, you are liable to do so again. Our main tool for change for the better is insight, especially about the influence of the past upon our present.

The early years are so influential because they are an extended period of extreme dependence on others for survival, much longer than any other species in the animal kingdom. To survive, we do our best to keep our parents, or whoever is caring for us, sweet. When small, we feel unconditional love for them and a great concern to make them happy. The most obvious tactic is to imitate; we all like it if others seem to agree with us and follow what we prefer. Whether our carers are chirpy or gloomy, we mirror it and that is what comes to seem natural.

We also absorb their skills and attitudes to give ourselves a feeling of control, safety and identity. To ingratiate ourselves and to compete with siblings and other children, we take the line of least resistance in adopting parental characteristics. At the most basic level, we identify with our parents in order to know who to be. We feel safest with the familiar, even if that was maltreatment.

Because we are already prone to being a certain way, we get stereotyped accordingly. Once placed in that box, it becomes ever harder for ourselves or those around us to think of our character in any other way – a self-fulfilling prophecy. The patterns of being bright or lively or moody become very ingrained.

During adolescence, we start forming romantic relationships, trying out different kinds of sexual partners. We begin the social networking that will ultimately be expressed in our professional careers. Whether leaving school young and getting a job, or continuing in education, each route leads to a specialization which is further narrowed by our choice of profession or university degree. All the time we are constantly making decisions based on our original family history, which restricts our alternatives and ingrains the patterns still further.

In our twenties and thirties the consolidation rigidifies. We are likely to pick a mate strongly influenced by what our opposite-sexed parent was like. The result is a family life in which we live out scenes from our original family drama with exquisite precision, incorporating scripts from our partner (hand-picked, remember, for his or her similarity to our father or mother). We will probably seek a career which is either a reflection of what our parents did, or a reaction to it.

How rich or poor our parents were, and their cultural preferences, are all strong influences on the details of these developments, like the sort of lifestyle we prefer or our taste in food, but affluence or its lack does not in itself affect how emotionally healthy we are. Our gender also has an effect, if only because our parents and wider society have such strong reactions to it. What is more, the kind of society we are in is a powerful influence – to take two startling examples, a Nigerian is six times less likely than an American to suffer a mental illness, and a Singaporean child is ten times less likely to be illiterate than a British one. Yet none of these things is as important to emotional health as our early care.

The greatest challenge is the fact that the 'you' who is reading these words and thinking about your childhood is doing so according to ways of thinking and feeling that were created by that childhood. To use a simple analogy, if you are wearing a pair of spectacles with the wrong lenses, everything you see will be distorted, however hard you strain your eyes. As the British psychoanalyst Ronald Laing put it, 'We are the veils that veil us from ourselves.' We have a huge loyalty to that veil, because it came from our parents and all too often, grandparents and great-grandparents. Consider the following example.

Gerald was raised in a large family by socially insecure parents. They impressed upon him the importance of honesty and authenticity, and yet they also covertly pressurized him to be a pleasing, compliant, upwardly mobile and socially successful boy. He developed a false persona, a carapace behind which he concealed his true emotions when in the company of others. The vicious twist was that he pretended to be real, in obeisance to the parental instruction to be authentic. Hence, he would tell teachers and bosses when he thought they were wrong, although it would have been better to keep quiet, or he would tell friends their faults without reference to what they could cope with hearing. In doing so, he would believe he was being authentic, whereas, in fact, he was merely living out his parents' beliefs, not his own true wishes or the demands of the real situation he was in. He followed his parents in confusing the unfailing expression of his true opinions in all situations with authenticity.

It was very confusing for him and he married a woman who shared this problem. Their children were presented with the same muddled message. On the one hand, they had to be true to themselves, on the other, they must conform to the conventions of their social class and gender. In due course, they married partners with the same confusing attributes, had children, and, lo and behold, there arose a fourth generation embarked on the same struggle of competing, paradoxical demands: to be both true and false. In this generation, however, one of them was able to escape the trap.

A youngest child, Emily, was less brainwashed by the family ideology. She moved away from her home town after attending university and was able to see with remarkable clarity how the trap had been set all those years ago. Not only was she able to grasp that her people-pleasing tendency was a false self, she realized that the family's intergenerational compulsion for speaking honestly was both self-destructive and a form of falsehood, because it was not something she had chosen for herself, it was simply a family tradition passed down the generations. With this insight, she set about building her own self, one which was truly authentic rather than a pretence thereof, whilst also developing a facade of her own which she could use to deal with situations that required tact and diplomacy, or even lies. She became far more emotionally healthy than any of her siblings or ancestors.

A key reason for her escape from the historic pattern was the accident of Emily's birth-order (she was the youngest of five), a big influence on us all, along with the nurture we experience before age six. We have to find ways as children to attract the love and resources of our parents. We seek niches that will enable us to do so, personae that mark us out.

If firstborn, we tend to take the line of least resistance, providing parents with what they want and siding with them. When the next child arrives the firstborn is quick to assert its prior claims and do his or her best to dominate. Since, as the firstborn, we are bigger and stronger, this makes us tend to be more self-assured. However, depending on how successful our younger siblings are in grabbing attention, we may be angry and vengeful at being supplanted. Behind the veneer of confidence there is liable to be considerable fear. As the oldest, we are likely to be roped into child-rearing tasks and be required to act as the responsible sibling. This makes us less keen on risk, more conservative, and anxious to conserve the status quo which preceded the birth of our siblings. Being a conscientious pupil at school is a simple way to curry favour with parents, if this is important to them.

By the time the lastborn comes along, many of the obvious niches for attracting parental love and investment are liable to have been taken. Given limited options, as a lastborn we may find our best strategy is to innovate and reject the status quo. Travel may appeal as a way of escaping from a family which has less to offer us, whilst also providing useful ideas on how to be different. At the same time, we may find that being altruistic and supportive is a way to pre-empt hostility from older, stronger siblings. This can make us a good team player.

As the youngest of five, much less of the family culture rubbed off on Emily. Once she reached university, she began to question the family's messy mixture of falsehood and authenticity. The veil that veiled her from herself was flimsier than that of her ancestors. She saw through it partly just from noticing that being false was making it hard for her to get close to anyone, but this clarity was also nurtured when a lecturer encouraged her interest in the novelist Jane Austen. From reading these books, rich in realism, irony and social commentary, Emily was able to conceptualize her family's mistaken presentation of a stark choice between frankness (often amounting to giving other people more information than they needed) and dissembling. Instead, she began trying out a more balanced approach, the kind found in emotionally healthy dealings with others.

Previously, when feeling insecure, she had been liable to become either jammed on 'transmit' or on 'receive'. In 'transmit' mode, she would be like someone who had taken cocaine, convinced that only what she was saying was of interest and right. Whether arguing about politics or the virtues of a TV programme, she would hold forth with an opinionated inflexibility. Equally, if in 'receive' mode, she would become compliant and ingratiating, agreeing with opinions that she really disputed, a chameleon. Now she became much better able to tolerate the notion of self and others' view of themselves, depending on the person and situation. She was able to remain herself and be assertive, yet listen to others and hear what they were really saying; her interactions were much more nuanced. Little by little she started finding friends she could speak openly to about matters that were troubling her, rather than always being the one others used as a sounding board. If she was sad or angry, she felt able not to conceal it, but only if that was appropriate. For, equally, she became much more cunning. She was able, as the emotionally healthy are, to keep quiet if saying something was not going to have any useful effect. With her friends, she ceased to be tactless. With her boss she became more artful, yet at the same time was less likely to be selling herself short by not asserting her rights. Instead of a self-destructive combination of falsehood and crassness, she became much more subtle, able to be herself and to adapt to the situation she was in.

An additionally liberating accident was the significance of Emily's gender. All parents react to their children's gender, but in her parents' case, they had longed particularly for a girl, after having had four boys. This special status gave her unusual freedom to challenge the established order.

Her story illustrates how much freer we are to move towards emotional health if the obstructions to it are a matter of family culture and events that occur largely after age six. To the extent that you have simply inherited a damaging family culture, and depending on your capacity to feel safe to challenge your parents in your mind, you can call that culture into question. As we shall see in the coming chapters, it is a bigger challenge to address earlier experiences, because, although they are vast, we have little conscious memory of them – but it is still possible.

But regarding your gender, birth order and the more or less explicit imperatives of your family culture, these factors are identifiable and can be addressed.

Exercise

Write a list of the attributes that were scripted for you. Then you can begin to challenge them. For example, before the next family gathering, write down the expectations that each of your parents and siblings will have of you. You might be seen as the bossy or shy or clever one, the girly girl or the tomboy, the driven man or the passive one. Instead of conforming to these stereotypes, try deliberately behaving in the opposite fashion. If nothing else, this experiment should be entertaining; but it might also give you some insights into ways of behaviour which have become routine, and which impede your emotional health.

Don't bow to genetic determinism

In Emily's case, perhaps the most important aspect of all was her refusal to accept the idea that the patterns in her family were an unchangeable genetic destiny (this was something that her relatives believed). Believing in genetic determinism is bad for your emotional health. There are a host of studies showing that – whether you are the child concerned, or the parent or teacher thereof – believing that a trait is predetermined by genes influences the child for the worse. But with the findings of the Human Genome Project, at last we have a solid scientific basis for dismissing this restrictive ideology and replacing it with one that will maximize our emotional health.

I will not pretend that it is easy to derive from one's life the freedom to live at first hand. Yet, in a sense, that is what we were put on this earth for: we exist to work towards greater emotional health, not to be happier or to reproduce our selfish genes. You can decide to continue to live in your established ways, endlessly repeating the past, believing yourself to be unchangeable, constantly getting back (and being crammed by others) into your box. Or you can challenge your status quo and your genes will do almost nothing to stand in your way. Yes, your childhood history, your friends and family, your society, they will have to be constantly confronted. But the first critical step towards emotional health is the conviction that through insight, you can colonize the past in your present, and start to live.

2. Living in the Present: A Sense of Self

There was a boy who excelled at school in every respect and went on to do the same at university. At the end of his second year he set off one morning to take an exam and disappeared. He was found twenty-four hours later, wandering around, completely lost. He was not just lost in the sense that he did not know which city he was in. He was lost existentially, did not feel he existed. Having developed an extraordinarily sophisticated and successful false self and lived behind it for two decades, his true self, the one experiencing his real needs, had become invisible to him. The problem was not just that his awareness of himself in social space had evaporated, his knowledge of such things as the name on his birth certificate. He also had lost track of who he was as a human being.

Having a weak identity – a fragile sense of self – makes it harder to live at first hand, in the present moment. If you do not know who you are, you become prone to pretences, to living 'as if' you are you, and to developing ways of coping that can be self-destructive. You may resort to game-playing (sometimes mistaken for playfulness), or striving for recognition and identity through achievements, to create meaning because nothing much feels very true or real. Equally, you may be prone to a hyperactive and hectic lifestyle, in order to distract yourself from the emptiness and loneliness of existing through a false self. This might be mistaken for vivacity. You may appear outwardly emotionally healthy, but in fact your identity is a pretence; you are not living in the present.

Inner identity

A weak sense of self evolves out of the way our needs are responded to by carers in our first year of life. Of course, social identity derives from one's nationality, family background and gender. But the inner aspect of identity, hard though it may be to believe, derives from our earliest relationships. In the first year, our experience is governed by the physical and the primitive, unmediated by language. Existence can be simply going from feeling hungry to feeling full up, from feeling cold to feeling warm, from feeling unloved to feeling loved. Love is expressed by the meeting of the physical needs. At this stage, there are weak boundaries between what exists within and what exists outside, between Me and Not-me. Sucking on a bottle or breast, we have no idea what milk is, only an experience of needing something and either getting it or not. We are completely powerless, unable even to sit up, let alone use words to convey our wishes. It's a vulnerable situation, potentially unbearable.

We depend wholly on the empathy of our carers to discern our needs. In this sense, the English psychoanalyst Donald Winnicott was right when he wrote that 'there is no such thing as a baby'. A baby only exists insofar as he has his sensations confirmed by the care he receives. If this happens thousands and thousands of times, in tiny ways over many months, he gradually gains a consis-

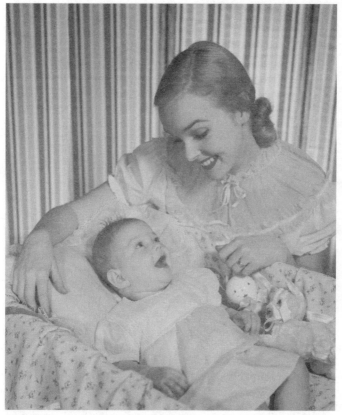

A baby only exists insofar as he has his sensations confirmed by the care he receives.

tent sense of what he wants, anchored in physical sensations, as opposed to what his carer wants him to want. Through these sensations, and the carer's smiles and cooing and other communications, his sense of self emerges. The carer gets some good little gags going with the baby, tiny routines unique to the two of them that a stranger could never provide, however responsive. This joyful intimacy also becomes the foundation of playfulness, authenticity and vivacity. Such a solid base can confer emotional health in the face of daunting subsequent adversities.

Take George, a 49-year old man from Shanghai, China. During the month I spent in that city interviewing about forty of its residents in 2004, he was the only one I met who had actually been cared for by his mother during the early years. Nearly everyone there was looked after by a grandmother or in nurseries, so that the more robust younger women, the mothers, could work. But in George's case, his mum gave up her job to be there at all times and was very loving. This provided a strong sense of self, which stood him in good stead for what was to come.

His father was a drunk. His mother hated him (his father) for a fecklessness which meant that the family was poor even by the standards of poor families in 1950s China, often starving. At school George was mocked for not having shoes to wear or any lunch. Although uneducated herself, his mother stressed the importance of schooling, whilst his father denigrated it.

When he was nineteen, as a result of the Cultural Revolution, George was sent off to be a labourer. He had to dig irrigation dykes to reclaim the land. He and the other labourers left their dormitory at six in the morning and walked for an hour to get to the job site.

Then began the digging and carrying of the soil. They were from the city and not used to such physical strain. The sludge was so slippery people often worked in bare feet, and in the winter it was freezing cold. They dug and carried until lunch, then went back to work, before the trudge home around 5 p.m.

Despite all these travails, George managed to learn English from a transistor radio (the Communist Party was transmitting lessons in the language at that time) and to get his hands on novels. When the Cultural Revolution ended he went on to university and has subsequently had a successful business career. But what is so startling is the way he radiates emotional health.

Despite his forty-nine years, he still has a full head of jet-black hair and only a slight paunch. He is a tremendously engaging fellow, warm, amusing and amused. Chinese people tend not to show a lot of emotion, displaying instead a flat, steady mood, whereas George is like an Italian. When he makes a point he waves his arms, his voice sometimes reaches contralto as he squeaks with amusement at some folly of Mao's regime. At other times, his face goes black with despair and his voice is as sad as an operatic tenor bemoaning the suicide of his beloved. He has a fiercely independent view of Chinese society and its history, and is a man of mature opinion. But when I met him he was also full of curiosity about what I thought, and could be a good listener. Above all, he was a delight to share a meal with, full of funny stories and friendliness, and excited just to be alive. His sense of self infused all of this, and easily overrode misfortunes which would have weighed heavily on someone who had not had such a nurturing mother.

Dissociation

The absence of the kind of care experienced by George has been proven to result in a diminished sense of self. As long ago as the 1940s it was noticed that orphans housed in impersonal institutions suffered physical and mental harm, known as 'hospitalism': lethargy, failure to develop the most basic social and mental skills, and extreme susceptibility to infections and disease. Those in orphanages did far better if relationships with individual carers were encouraged. It was not the sensory deprivation of the children's cribs, the lack of toys or stimulation, that damaged the neglected babies, nor was it simply the absence of their mother. What was critical was the presence of someone who knew the baby intimately and understood his or her specific needs, capacities, idiosyncrasies and vulnerabilities.

At least half of men and one third of women raised in institutions have depleted selves, with the likelihood of this occurring increasing according to how young the child was when poor parenting was experienced. But the same is true of those raised by unempathic parents at home. Researcher John Ogawa and his American colleagues followed 168 children from birth to the age of nineteen, measuring the quality of the care they received throughout childhood, to test whether early maltreatment correlated with problems in later life. The parents were selected because they were at high risk of depriving or abusing the children. In particular, the impact of early parental care on dissociation was measured.

Dissociation is a distinctive sign of a weak sense of self, entailing a variety of amnesiac mental tactics for evading painful realities, like failing to notice things, or forgetting or refusing to acknowledge them. Dissociated people also escape from the present by becoming distantly absorbed in a single aspect of the inner or outer world, for instance, gazing hypnotically at a pattern in the wallpaper, or disappearing into fantasies in the company of others. There may be depersonalization, in which events are experienced as if by a third party, disconnected from one's own body or feelings. At its most extreme, the dissociated person may develop different sub-personalities into which they escape. (In some cases this is the precursor of schizophrenia, a state in which you may actually believe that you are someone else, like Jesus Christ.)

Ogawa demonstrated that the degree to which care was neglectful or abusive before the age of two predicted whether a person would suffer from dissociation seventeen years later. Despite the fact that an enormous number of influences intervened between the early care and the measurement of the 19-year-old personality, its substantial impact was proven. Those in the sample who were only maltreated after infancy – whether between the ages of two and four, or in middle or later childhood – were significantly less likely to be dissociated at nineteen: the earlier the maltreatment, the greater the likelihood of symptoms. Genetic factors appeared to play no part; the baby's temperament immediately after birth or at three months did not predict how they turned out.

Ogawa also showed that if a child had developed a strong sense of self early on, through empathic care, it was more resilient and far less likely to become dissociated when faced by traumas in later life. Being uncertain of who they are, the weak-selfed require less severe and less frequent trauma to make them doubt their reality, compared to those with a stronger sense of self. Because their psychic boundaries are fragile, they are more prone to dissociative escape from intolerable realities. The stronger-selfed can manage to remain themselves, as George did, through thick and thin. This is suggested by another study which showed that 22-year-old adults had more insights about themselves and were more respectful of others' autonomy, if their mothers had been sensitive in caring for them during the first year of their lives.

Of course, severe maltreatment after infancy does, in itself, greatly increase the risk of a weak sense of self. It is now an accepted fact (based on twenty-three different studies) that at least half of people with schizophrenia suffered childhood abuse, mostly sexual. Such abuse actually impedes brain growth, so that a woman who was sexually abused as a girl has 5 per cent less of a key part of the brain (the hippocampus) than one who was not. The earlier the abuse, the closer the familial relationship of abuser to abused (family members are far more harmful) and the more extreme the form of the abuse (sexual penetration being most damaging), the greater the number of sub-personalities developed and the more severe the symptoms of damage to the self. Whilst better early care can allow the sufferer to carve out some elements of emotional health, such abuse is a major independent cause of a weak self.

Emotional health with a weak self

The cost of a weak sense of self to emotional health is large, although, thankfully, not necessarily permanent. I once interviewed an American called Henry, a man whose mother believed herself to be the present Queen of England and had great difficulty in tuning into him as a baby. His home was a Petri dish for craziness.

His uncle lived with the family and believed that the Second World War was still going on, probably suffering from post-traumatic stress disorder from his time as a soldier. He would beat Henry and rub salt into his eyes (he also used to attack the Asian postman, believing he was a Japanese soldier). When Henry was only five years old, his older brother's idea of an amusing jape was to wake him up with spooky howling, wearing a white sheet and holding a torch beneath his chin to create a spectral luminescence, impersonating a mad butcher-ghost, while holding up a meat cleaver. When he was placed in a children's home, Henry was relieved to escape from his family home, only to suffer a new regime of extreme deprivation and physical abuse there.

Eventually returned to his crazy childhood home in his late teens, Henry (understandably) began to have delusions. Various voices in his head sought to convince him that he must buy guns and shoot as many people as possible. Interestingly, though, he had enough sense of self to resist these ideas, so he made a deal with himself that he hoped would preclude his committing such a massacre: he would only do it if he won the state lottery. Unfortunately, to his astonishment, this was exactly what happened. But on receipt of several thousand dollars he still did not act, and instead created another obstruction.

At the time he believed that one radio station was God speaking to him, while another was Satan. He made a pact that if the satanic station played the song 'Another One Bites the Dust' he would do the killings. When that happened, his resistance was overcome. With (shocking) ease he purchased a variety of dangerous weapons (he just walked into a gun shop and said 'I want the gun that shoots the most bullets'). But the interesting thing was that even then he had enough sense of self to act in a relatively emotionally healthy way. Instead of going to the nearest highly populated public place and blasting away, he ran through his home, killing his mother, uncle and brother. Whilst murder is never a sign of emotional health as such, once you understand the full context, these particular murders can be said to display a certain amount of emotional health: his family were the historical and present cause of his madness; they were a far healthier target, from an emotional-health point of view, than random members of the public.

What struck me as remarkable when I met Henry was how very emotionally healthy he now seemed. This was some ten years after the killings and he had been the beneficiary of a superb therapeutic regime, unhampered by psychiatric medication. He spoke with calmness and clarity throughout. He was insightful, and despite the unrelenting darkness of what he had to say, delivered it with a playfulness in his choice of words and with a dark humour. For instance, when relating the move to a children's home, he painted a hilarious picture of the way the director of that institution presented the place to his social worker as a loving, safe environment, only to turn into a monster as soon as she had left. He dealt with me skilfully, never becoming annoyed by my more or less ham-fisted, insensitive questions, always gently indicating that he would tell me what I wanted to know all in good time.

One striking detail did emerge from my questions, however. It turned out that his mother was not the only person who cared for him as a baby. During the periods when she was too disturbed to cope, a loving and sane relative often took over. That explained the strength of his sense of self, which had proven sufficient to survive gargantuan assaults on his grasp of reality.

I do not know where he is now (the interview was done in 1988) but I would lay money on the likelihood that Henry is a tremendously constructive member of a community, brimming with emotional health and spreading it around. The reason that the vast majority of people who have endured his mixture of infantile deprivation and subsequent abuse do not turn out like Henry is that they have not had his good fortune of being partly cared for by a loving, responsive person. It is very rare for this to happen in such families. If parents and relatives are deeply disturbed, the maltreatment tends to occur at all stages, more or less. As a result, the person has nothing to fall back on, no fragments of self on which to build. Whilst very intensive and skilled therapy can help the person to construct some self in later life, alas very few people can afford it, and it is hardly ever available from conventional mental health (or prison) services. However, therapy is not the only answer for those lacking a sense of self.

How to address a weak self

Almost any field of endeavour – a project or interest that demands time and attention – can be used as a way to cope with a weak self, some more conducive to emotional health than others. Alas, the commonest are self-destructive or unhelpful; coping is not the same as treating.

Substance abuse provides a form of self-coherence and powerful bodily sensations, addressing the electrochemical lacks originating in infancy. The sensations following ingestion of heroin, for example, can be very similar, in experiential terms, to those of being fed as a baby. The drugs are more reliable than an unresponsive or erratic mother and we can trust them to deliver instant and powerful feelings every time. They provide a reason to live, something someone with a weak sense of self is always searching for (most powerfully evoked in the Velvet Underground song 'Heroin'). There is a reassuring, meaningful narrative which revolves around the getting of the drugs and the money to pay for them (as evoked in the Velvet Underground song 'Waiting for the Man'). Alas, this latter often entails criminality – often prostitution in young women, and theft in young men.

However, hard work and exceptional achievement can also provide a self, and be every bit as addictive as heroin, producing electrochemical changes in the body which compensate for infantile lacks. I have interviewed about a hundred famous people from a wide variety of fields who are clearly seeking success in order to compensate for feelings of powerlessness and worthlessness dating back to infancy. The buzz of heightened cortisol experienced when making massive financial deals or performing to huge audiences can confer the same fundamental sense of meaning; likewise the floods of brain chemicals, like dopamine or oxytocin, that can come from being kowtowed to by compliant employees or worshipped by fans.

The successful frequently operate through a sophisticated false self. It creates a tragic spiral of loneliness. The more successful we become, the more people relate to the persona we have created. In the case of famous artists of all kinds, when strangers point to them in the street or come up and ask 'Are you ___?' they experience a temporary boost to their self-esteem and a reminder of who they are. Many of them are never far from feeling as lost as the man with whom this chapter began, who was found wandering the streets not knowing his name. Having felt invisible as infants, these people are given a fleeting sense of identity by being recognized. But it does not fix the basic problem, as they become increasingly liable to confuse the persona they have created with their true self. Intimates are either alienated – complaining that their starry husband or wife or sibling is no longer the person they once knew – or else start relating to the famous persona too.

Something very similar tends to happen to top business performers, except it is people within the organization and profession who relate to the persona. Such business tycoons tend to have minimal private lives, with little time available for family and friends, so their social exchanges are restricted to people over whom they have direct power. The employees ingratiate themselves to – and never challenge – the false self, and the true self gets lost.

Of course, it is not only the exceptionally successful to whom these factors apply. Those of us with difficulties in our selfhood are to be found at all levels of society. Through accidents of our history we may not be inclined to use dynamism or cleverness to compensate for weak selves. Some of us may simply have what psychiatrists call personality disorders, tending to be febrile in our emotions, very self-focused (narcissistic) and wild in our ideas. These traits tend to poison our personal and professional lives.

This is not to say that weak-selfed people have no elements of emotional health at all. The weak-selfed may use playfulness as a way of skating on the surface of life, perhaps being highly entertaining in their facetiousness or creating amusing characters through mimicry when socializing. They can have slightly manic bouts of vivacity – that person you know at work who sometimes becomes a very lively contributor to projects, while at other times barely says a word. These individuals can have astonishing insight into others, because the boundaries between themselves and others are weaker and they see people's unconscious thoughts without trying. Alas, although they may have occasional shafts of insight into themselves, they are usually less able to see inwards. Likewise, they have difficulty achieving two-way, fluid communication. Either they are needily trying to make their point or to be the centre of attention, or they are hiding away and silent.

We nearly always have some healthy components which we can build on, and playfulness and vivacity are good starting points for the weak-selfed. However, it is important to differentiate between genuine playfulness and vivacity and counterfeit versions.

Play is a pretend state, where a person enjoys treating an imaginary scenario as real. It is one of the most rewarding of human attributes, usually entailing humour. Whether putting on accents or dialects in telling amusing stories, or allowing ourselves to exaggerate reality to tell a surreal story, we enjoy it richly. Play is at its most obvious in small children, their greatest source of pleasure. It is closely allied to vivacity, a heightened sense of being alive, often accompanied by a buoyant, active frame of mind. As we move through school and towards adulthood, playfulness can get redirected into Machiavellian gameplaying, and vivacity can be replaced by hyperactive, compulsive speech and action. For those working in professions which require marketing of self and products, these characteristics can be useful; likewise for anyone working in the arts or professions, such as the law, which demand performance. But they should not be mistaken for the real thing.

It is nonetheless possible, through one's work, to gain a measure of selfhood and, thereby, some emotional health. The five-book sequence about the fictional life of Patrick Melrose, by the English novelist Edward St Aubyn, is a model for how to carve superb literature out of horrendous maltreatment.

Melrose was abused by his father, a man of sadism and some psychopathy. St Aubyn has revealed that the father was based on his own. Melrose wrestles throughout the books with a lack of self. As a youth he becomes a fanatical drug user. He struggles to stay sane, as voices in his head plague him. Free from drugs, he moves onto alcohol, and is unable to resist sexual infidelities. Yet as the books progress it becomes apparent that Melrose's plight is no different at a fundamental level from our own; the books raise general questions of the greatest importance. They expose the universality of the tendency to either robotically reproduce, or react against, the care we received as children. Whether from an affluent home or a poor one, whether hideously mistreated or just averagely neglected, this is the human predicament. In a triumphant end to the books, St Aubyn provides a very moving, satisfying and optimistic basis for seeking independent volition.

Most striking of all, St Aubyn has discussed the role that the actual writing of the books played in his own development. Whilst by no means suggesting that it was therapy, he made a Faustian pact with himself to either tell this story, or kill himself. His purpose was not to unburden himself of guilt or to transfer his bad feelings to the reader, it was simply to create a beautiful work of art which illuminates the human quest for free choice.

In the view of newspaper reviewers, he succeeded. He created literature of astonishing virtuosity, exquisitely written, and filled with insights into the human condition. In doing so, he may have achieved some sense of self, because, just as Melrose discovers that insight into his motives and immediate actions is the only way for him to avoid re-enacting his miserable childhood history, so the same is true for St Aubyn. The problem of selfhood does not get solved, but it is substantially reduced.

Individualism

Community and group membership can provide another important potential route to greater emotional health for the weak-selfed. However, in developed nations, our tendency towards individualism can get in the way. There has been a huge shift towards it since the Second World War, accelerating in recent years. In the individualist society, identity is achieved first through education, and subsequently through career. 'What is your job?' becomes the first question a stranger wants answered. By contrast, in the collectivist society, it is 'who are your parents?' In the latter case, identity is conferred upon you by virtue of your family, your position in it, your gender and your society's suppositions about who such a person should be.

For example, in 1978 I spent three months studying the inhabitants of Borbon, a village a small distance up a river on the west coast of Ecuador in South America. Who you were there depended first and foremost upon your gender.

If female, you were likely to begin having children as a teenager. Caring for your offspring and scraping together a living became your daily preoccupation. Although your partner or husband might stay around for a year or two, he would be liable to travel up and down the river, or even farther afield, in search of work. Men could not be relied upon to support the family at all times, so the women needed to cultivate crops and keep chickens, as well as acting as matriarchs, often supported by sisters and mothers. The men also began parenthood in their teenage years, but would expect to father children by several different women in different villages over the years.

The potential for the kind of individuality that is such an important aspiration of people in developed nations was considerably less in Borbon. This was partly a result of the material conditions. There was minimal difference in the wealth between different households. Your individualism would not be expressed by your possessions. Whilst there was a generator producing electricity for a handful of buildings for some hours of the day, in the villagers' homes there were none of the electrical goods we take for granted, like fridges, dishwashers or televisions. On top of that, anyone wanting to challenge the social norms would be given very short shrift. A woman who started behaving like a man, for example, largely ignoring her children and travelling up and down the river in search of work, would be ostracized. Likewise, a man trying to behave like a woman. Not that anyone I met showed any sign of trying to rebel in these or other ways. With only small variations, everyone in that community received only very basic care in the early years. Yet because of the very strong collectivist social system, this did not result in personality disorders in later life. The lack of pressure for individualism reduced the damage that such early neglect would have brought in the West.

On the whole, emerging or developing nations are still strongly collectivist, whereas European and English-speaking ones are more individualistic. It is no coincidence that the highest rates of personality disorder are in ultra-individualistic America – many times higher than in Asian nations.

For the weak-selfed person, being an individual is hard. You have to decide who to be, what to do, and if you lack self, that is a huge demand, making resorting to drugs or alcohol or a workaholic lifestyle more likely. That is not to say that all collectivist societies are better for emotional health. In developed nations in the 1950s, both women and people from low-income homes were forced to stay in their boxes, suppressing their creativity and authenticity. Collectivism can be oppressive, but it does have some useful lessons for the weak-selfed person living in a developed nation.

Membership of groups, perhaps based on hobbies or ethical beliefs, promotes emotional health. Just being part of a tennis club or doing weekly line-dancing lessons will lessen your sense of rootlessness and emptiness, as will meeting friends in the pub. What is more, people who have a weekly religious practice are significantly less likely to suffer mental illness. Whether it be yoga, meditation or conventional religion, simply by being part of a community with shared ethical beliefs or rituals, you will gain identity. It is not going to fix a deep lack of a sense of self. But it can help to confer a sense of who you are and how to live your life, providing a foundation for vivacity and playfulness, and helping to foster authenticity.

Just being part of a tennis club or doing weekly line-dancing lessons will lessen your sense of rootlessness and emptiness.

As we saw in the cases of Henry (who murdered several of his family members) and Edward St Aubyn (the novelist), a weak self does not guarantee lack of emotional health. Even in very extreme situations, there is always the possibility of volition.

3. Fluid, Two-Way Relationships

Jean-Paul Sartre's play *Huis Clos* (No Exit) starts with just one character on the stage, puzzled as to where he is. Another arrives, then four more, all equally bewildered. It becomes clear that in each case, one of the people there is the embodiment of everything one of the others loathes. At last one of the characters realizes what has happened: they have died and gone to hell. 'Hell is other people,' he observes.

This is not so for the emotionally healthy; for them, other people are among their greatest blessings. Because they are able to listen as well as assert their views, because they can present a front to the world which largely reflects their true feelings, because they are usually neither paranoid nor depressed, other people enrich their lives, and vice versa, personally and professionally. Alas, for the rest of us, other people are a challenge to emotional health. Friends let us down or become a drag on our resources, with their endless stories of woe or tendency to repeat themselves. Colleagues frustrate, betray or outwit us, thwarting our designs. Lovers and spouses interfere, torment, deprive or deplete. Children are worrying and upsetting. Siblings and parents put us back in our boxes, or make huge demands.

Attachment patterns

Of particular importance in determining whether other people are heaven or hell for us is the period when we are toddlers, between six months and three years of age. Those of us whose carers were unresponsive, or who were cared for by a different person from one day to the next, often have what is called an insecure pattern of attachment. This is true of about 30 per cent of children and at least 40 per cent of adults. If we felt rejected by our early care, we become avoidant. We are often angry people and prone to reject others, getting our rejection in first because we expect to be rebuffed by friends, teachers, employers and lovers. Alternatively, if we felt abandoned by carers, then we bring the assumption that this will always be the case to those relationships, expressed in clingy neediness, and sometimes mixed with a perplexing reluctance to engage if the other person does respond. Finally, if the care was chaotic and downright disturbing (actual maltreatment, like abuse) we bring a muddling mixture of rejection, neediness and disconnection to our relationships.

This is well illustrated by the contrasting tales of two men.

The first is Dave, in his early sixties, a vibrant, delightful example of emotional health. Dave is of Asian origin, born and raised in Kenya. His father managed to build up a small fruit-growing business outside Nairobi. It was touch-and-go, with the crop wiped out by droughts and diseases on several occasions. But the imaginativeness of his father and his constant ability to find solutions made a deep impression on Dave, inspiring him when he hit trouble himself at various points later in his life. He felt loved by his father, an endearingly warm and humorous man. His mother cared for him as a young child with a passionate affection that was evident in the warm, considerate way Dave related to me, six decades later: the sort of mother you would want as a friend.

Dave's father was successful enough to pay for him to go to university in London, where he subsequently trained as an accountant. A Muslim, his parents arranged a marriage with a woman from a good family. Dave had always wanted to set up his own business and managed to get backing. Now came the toughest time of his life. Nearly strangled at birth by a recession, Dave's business barely survived, even with him working seven days a week. Alas, his wife's family were unimpressed. They put pressure on her to leave such a 'loser' and Dave could not persuade her otherwise. Given that he has since become enormously successful, he might be forgiven for adopting a triumphant tone when reporting these events to me. Instead, he looked down into his coffee, a sad frown of misery on his face as he remembered that time. He pleaded with her to persevere, and for a few days after he had failed, felt desperate. He found solace at his local mosque.

His marriage over, his business survived and flourished. It teaches workplace skills, often to relatively low-income people hoping to better themselves, and Dave is passionate about its social value. With other entrepreneurs you might be forgiven for suspecting that this is a front, but not Dave. He is genuinely excited by the idea of education and loves making educational presentations himself. He also speaks with passion of trying to create a working environment in which his employees have a good time. He is not a managerial control freak, having trained others to take on many of the key executive roles, and truly delegating power to them. But what is most indicative that money is not Dave's lodestar is the enjoyment he has taken in helping the Muslim community in the northern British city where he lives. After his divorce, he realized he knew hardly anyone well, so he made a point of doing community work, which brought him into dependent and substantial relationships with flesh-and-blood human beings.

He founded an organization that supports the Muslim community, buying a local amateur soccer club and building it up. He sees it as vital to commit his own time and energy to the project, as well as his money. Although he has set himself the goal of creating a £1-billion company, he does not seem obsessed by it. He works only forty to fifty hours a week and intends to start cutting down, passing the management over to younger people, and spending more time on his community work. If he raises his own wages it is only ever in proportion to a corresponding raise received by his employees.

A few years after his marriage ended, Dave remarried and he and his wife adopted children. He speaks of them with real affection, and is able to describe their lives in such detail that it is clear that he is not dissembling when he claims to be involved in their nurture. He does not seem motivated by conspicuous consumption – his clothing looks like that of any middle-class football supporter, his car is a bog-standard saloon.

At the heart of Dave is his secure pattern of attachment, derived from his parents' loving responsiveness. It explains why he thinks the best of people until they give him reason to suppose otherwise. He does not expect others to let him down or to reject him. If it happens, he properly mourns the loss and then can move on. If he

Money is not Dave's lodestar; he founded an organization that supports the Muslim community, buying a local amateur soccer club.

becomes isolated, he is able to engage with others to form enduring and mutually valuable relationships. Hell is not other people; they are the foundation of the meaning in his life and of his emotional health. After our meeting, I felt optimistic and cheerful, uplifted.

Contrast Dave with Archie, a convicted football hooligan whom I interviewed in prison. He was capable of shocking violence, thinking nothing of throwing darts into a crowded bar just for amusement. From early childhood his father frequently hit him, rarely with good reason or adequate explanation. His mother's attitude to him was cold and neutral. This childhood left him with severe difficulties when it came to being emotionally dependent on others. He was especially impoverished in his capacity to form satisfying relationships with women. Because his choice of words is so revealing, I shall present some of the transcript from our interview.

Q: Did you form any lasting relationships with women at all?
A: No, no. I never. Couldn't. I had girlfriends, like, well not girlfriends really, they were just what do you call them? 'Dodgy birds,' like. Definite leg-over, whenever you wanted one that you liked, you could get one. I didn't want to get emotionally attached to anyone.

Q: How did it go with your wife?
A: I was just fed up with it . . . it will sound crazy, but I got more kicks out of fighting than I did out of, you know, being with her. In a way, she was getting up my nose because she

was interfering with what I wanted to do. Instead of wasting my energy on sex with her, I was reserving it for fighting.

Archie was a man who dared not give or receive love, who felt empty and desperately lonely. He actually preferred violence to sex as a means for achieving emotional contact or excitement in this psychic desert. Anthony Storr, an English psychoanalyst, has given a vivid description of the dilemma faced by individuals for whom emotional contact is both a threat and a desperate necessity:

> Although, like all of us, they passionately long for love, they have so deep a mistrust of other human beings that any really intimate relation with another appears to them to be dangerous. . . [The schizoid] is thus faced with a perpetual dilemma. To deny the need for love is to enclose himself in a prison of isolation in which he is likely to be overtaken by a sense of sterile futility. To accept love is to place himself in a position of dependence so humiliating that he feels himself to be despicably weak in relation to the person who is offering it.

The schizoid reacts with malevolent hatred to those who help and like him, for these are the very people who most threaten to burst the bubble of unreality and detachment with which he keeps others at a distance. The hostility that the threat of emotional contact evokes is often projected onto the very person most offering sympathy and warmth, who is then attacked. If, as a result, the other person becomes hostile, the schizoid can withdraw behind the safe glaze of an icy coldness. It is preferable because he fears he will annihilate or be annihilated, that his very existence is at stake.

Archie had many Schizoid features.

Archie: Bodily contact: I didn't like it, I didn't want her [his wife] near me . . . I felt trapped . . . I said to myself a long time ago that I wouldn't get emotionally involved, and I happened to get emotionally involved with her and I didn't like the feelings.

Q: What were they?
A: Really they were everything sort of alien to me, you know, the whole chemistry workings had gone haywire, I wasn't used to things like that, like being cuddled and I'd never been cuddled before, you know, things like that.

Q: Didn't your mum cuddle you?
A: No, not really . . . the only contact I had has been physical and violent. Anything sort of smoochy, even dancing with a bird, I didn't like. I used to go to the discos, didn't used to dance, I used to stand at the bar and drink and wait for a fight to erupt. I didn't want to dance, only 'dance' in a different manner! My wife annoyed me a lot at certain times – but instead of hitting her like I felt like doing, I would go out and pick a fight.

Q: You'd go out and hit someone else instead?
A: Just pick anyone.

Q: Do you think that's what was happening earlier on as well, instead of hitting your father, and I think your mother – more than you realise – you hit other people, often strangers?
A: I think, yeah . . . you've hit (*sic*) a good point there! I used to take out my anger on her . . . no, I laugh about it, I joke about it, but it is serious, yeah. I've got to look at the funny side of things, because if I look on the sad side of things, I'd probably sit down and cry.

Q: Do you think you'd even attack yourself?
A: No, I'd just go and cry, and I don't intend to either.

Anthony Storr has also proposed that middle-class schizoids often channel their feelings of powerlessness and destructiveness into becoming unassailably successful. Their success draws people close to them who would normally be put off by their lack of personal warmth and humanity, easing the burden of their solitude. However, professional peers or employees cannot provide true intimacy.

Of course, middle-class schizoids very rarely use physical fighting in a public place as a way of achieving 'contact'. Archie expressed his schizoid mentality through his choice of profession but, being an uneducated working-class man, he could not use power, status or wealth to manipulate ideas or people to act as he wished; at least, not living people.

Archie: I had a good job. I was an embalmer. A great job, that was.

Q: You enjoyed being an embalmer?
A: Yeah, I worked on my own.

Q: What does an embalmer do?
A: His main objective is to preserve the body for the family to come and view it. You pump the blood out and put embalming fluid in and put a bit of make-up on. Great, you know what I mean? You've got no one to back-chat you and give you any hassle, you know. I found that really great. I lost the poxy job through drinking and driving. I was gutted.

Q: Is that your ideal relationship with another person, that the other person is dead?
A: Yeah, there was no one to give me any lip, know what I mean? And no one to boss me about and I done my own thing.

Q: Did you feel close to these bodies?
A: No, not really. In a way I've been dead inside for a great number of years, and seeing them bodies was nothing really, nothing to me. I've got a good nickname – the lads at Millwall [the football club Archie supported, notorious in the 1980s for its violent fans, Archie among them] call me Dr Death – sort of suited me well.

Despite everything, it is notable that Archie did have some emotionally healthy features. There was a verve in his use of language and a playfulness, such as when he punned that I had 'hit' on a good point. However, it is plain to see how his early years sent him on a completely different trajectory along the tree of emotional health from Dave. At the heart of his life was a void, one created by the lack of love in his infancy and as a toddler, subsequently exacerbated by his father's cruelty. He was so insecure in his pattern of attachment that he could not risk depending on anyone, and his rage towards his parents for how they let him down dominated his waking life. It is impossible for us to sustain much emotional health when we are so distanced from, scared of and aggressive towards others. Yet even someone as fragile as Archie can become more secure. A stable relationship with a therapist has been proven to increase security. And then there is always the potential provided by intimate friendships . . . and by lovers.

Romantic relationships

Insecurity is but one of many distortions from the past that we bring to relationships, and which challenge emotional health. At its simplest, we may learn bad habits from parents, like a tendency to interrupt others or to be shy and secretive. A more complex scenario emerges if parents repeatedly placed you in situations where whatever you did was wrong, a 'double bind'. You approach your mother to kiss her hello, she backs off. So you pull away, but then she asks 'Aren't you going to kiss your mother hello?'. If you kiss her, it's wrong, if you do not kiss her it's wrong. Such behaviour from intimates can drive you crazy, and there is a whole range of such behaviours which we may have been taught. The most obvious expressions of them are in our romantic lives. As soon as we embark on sexual relationships, we demonstrate an uncanny knack for creating trouble for ourselves.

For example, parental separation can send girls down troubled relationship branches at a young age. On average, a girl whose father left the parental home before her tenth birthday comes into puberty six months earlier than one from an intact family. Early pubescence strongly predicts starting sex young. This in turn not only significantly predicts an increased risk of various medical problems, like uterine cancer and sexual diseases, it also predicts lower academic performance and a higher likelihood of emotional problems. It also risks teenage pregnancy and subsequently unstable relationships with men. The past in this sort of girl's present sends her along a low branch on the tree of emotional health, unless, that is, she is able to spot that it is her father's departure that is leading her to use her precocious nubility in ways that create trouble for her.

Because our relationship with our opposite-sexed parent is so influential in determining what we find attractive in others, we have a lamentable tendency to repeat the past, picking partners who duplicate the behaviours of our parents. Disentangling this mess is a major challenge for marital therapists, who all too often focus on the pattern of communication between the partners, rather than their individual histories. If divorce or separation follows, we are liable to go out and find someone just like our first partner. That is one reason why divorcees who remarry are much more likely to get divorced again.

To top it all, there is a strong tendency for emotionally unhealthy folk to seek each other out. If at age sixteen a person is prone to depression and anxiety, then they are much more likely to get divorced in later life. As the depressed and anxious tend to marry each other, the problem is multiplied by two.

How to improve your relationships

That the emotionally healthy tend to marry one another as well is little consolation for the vast majority of us who find ourselves more or less in the fixes described. But that is a good place to start, for those who have not yet had children: try, as much as possible, to become emotionally healthy before you start reproducing. What is more, if you can also persuade someone more emotionally healthy than you to share your life, so much the better, their health will rub off on you.

For those who are already in a relationship and have children, and who feel that their emotional health is ailing, there are three vital steps towards more fluid relationships and, consequently, emotional health:

1. Look at your own childhood

The first is to reflect long and hard about how your own childhood has coloured your choice of partner and to understand that this does not mean that your partner shares every trait of your own mother or father. That your husband, for instance, shares your father's tendency to lose his temper if the washing-up is not done should not prevent you from noticing that, unlike your father, he is an enthusiastic cook and approaches the task of food shopping with equal ardour. Between you, you have to start a dialogue about how your pasts are colouring your present, to prune the psychic shrubbery and build relationships which break the past patterns.

2. Accept that separation is the last resort

The second step – painful though it may be – is to accept that now you have children, there must be very persuasive reasons if you are to separate or divorce. In the darkest moments, of course you will consider leaving your partner; at moments of greatest anger you may even threaten one another with just this. But before you go any further down that road, you need to grasp the scale of the wreckage that will be caused by the resulting car crash. Remember, bad experiences in adulthood are twice as likely if a person's parents separated or divorced when he or she was a child: on the whole, separation or divorce will be damaging to your children. Looked at more selfishly, divorcees themselves often suffer grievously. They not only have much higher rates of cancer, alcoholism and heart disease, with lower life expectancy, but are also much more prone to misery. This was proven most dramatically by a study of over 8,000 mothers of small children living with a partner. The quality of the woman's relationship with her partner and whether she was depressed were measured. Depression levels were reassessed again twelve months later, and the startlingly bad news was that over half of mothers who had broken up with their partners were liable to be more depressed afterwards than when first interviewed. This proves that a significant number of mothers in a lousy relationship feel even lousier when it ends. It is reminiscent of the joke at the end of Woody Allen's film

A significant number of mothers in a lousy relationship feel even lousier without it.

Annie Hall. A man goes to his therapist and says 'My wife thinks she's a chicken.' The shrink asks 'So why do you stay with her?' and he replies 'I need the eggs.' We seem to need each other's foibles, including the bad bits.

3. Seek more intimacy

The third and most vital step towards emotional health is to seek more intimacy in your life – and by that I do not mean 'have an affair'. Whilst an affair may be the solution for some people, for most it only makes matters worse. It is important to understand that modern life severely depletes our relationships. Studies comparing people in the 1950s and 1960s with the present day prove that we tend to have many, many more friends (accelerated by the likes of Facebook, email and the internet) but far fewer intimates. Yes, a therapist may be part of that answer, and a marital therapist may be needed too (make sure it is one who is willing to focus primarily on your childhood histories, rather than tinkering with the way you argue). But even more important may be to recapture the network of intimates which you may have belonged to at school or university, but which your subsequent life has dispersed.

Relationships, particularly playful and intimate ones, are crucial for emotional health, and vice versa. It's a two-way street. To find your way back down the branch of isolation to the main tree trunk, and onwards and upwards towards something more lively and satisfying may entail retracing your steps to old friends, as well as seeing the potential of everyone around you, including strangers. This often entails disentangling sex from friendship. Modern life gives us the illusion that sex is a commodity, a fix that can salve loneliness. But as sex addicts can testify, the equation is false.

In 2004 I interviewed a married woman in her mid-twenties. She had a splendid husband, to whom she was fanatically unfaithful. She had a delightful son, who was cared for by a nanny. During our interviews, she made several attempts to persuade me to sleep with her. It was abundantly clear that she was conflating the uniting of our bodies with a feeling of emotional closeness. Compulsively promiscuous, the more men she had sex with, the more desperate she felt, since physical closeness only left her more emotionally isolated. Her story is ultimately uplifting, however, because she has subsequently come to see how her early years left her feeling unloved, and that sex will never deal with that problem. Now she is able to appreciate that she is extremely fortunate to have her husband and child, and that what she needed was emotionally healthy relationships which provided real sustenance – playfulness rather than flirtation, and sustained intimacy rather than physical proximity.

Whether at work or at home, if relationships are a source of pain and frustration you should look within yourself. You probably cannot change the kind of person your partner is, but once you identify your own relationship patterns, you can change yourself. Hell does not have to be other people, if you can sort yourself out. For the emotionally healthy, other people are heaven.

4. Authenticity in Our Careers

The great majority of emotionally healthy people do not have high-flying or all-consuming careers; they are not workaholics. In most cases they just have jobs, not careers at all, working in order to live rather than living in order to work. They earn in order to have enough money to meet their real needs – food or housing. They may find their work challenging and absorbing, socially entertaining and enriching; enjoyable and fulfilling. But there is no great hankering to rise up a hierarchy and get paid more or have more power; they are happy with their job as, say, a checkout assistant or librarian or primary-school teacher.

Before that, at school, these individuals did not learn in order to earn praise and, in the longer-term, a high income. They regarded education as a means for acquiring skills and knowledge, which interested and benefited them. It was not a way of beating others, proving their superiority and enabling them to obtain enviable wealth, power or status. It enabled them to remain authentic in their education and their career. Since these domains – education and career – take up so much of our lives, how we approach them is a vital part of being authentic.

Many people constantly yearn for better grades during their education, however well they do. Subsequently, in the workplace, they cannot have too much pay or too much status. This is not so for

When it comes to achievement in the workplace, the emotionally healthy have a well-developed concept of enough.

the emotionally healthy. When it comes to achievement, they have a well-developed concept of enough. Professionally, they are satiable. They do not constantly compare themselves to others, or feel the need to keep up with the Joneses.

Authenticity in our careers

The kind of careers these 'authentic' people have, such as those examples given above, may seem dull at first. Although they are statistically unusual as people, their measurable achievements are often unexceptional. Some do have great talents but are reluctant to commit their whole lives to them. Geraldine, now aged twenty-eight, is a splendid example of this kind. She is one of the most emotionally healthy people I have ever met. Her story brightly illuminates the causes of healthy attitudes to careers.

At school she did well, although feeling no urge to work very hard. She describes her grades as 'decent', sufficient to get her to the good university she had in mind. Whilst she says she could have got 'fantastic grades' if she had worked 'extremely hard', she was 'happy going along as I was'. Her younger sister was more academic because she had a 'bigger brain' and now has a successful computer-software company. Geraldine shows no signs of having been competitive with her sister. This was partly because Geraldine was the athletic one, an extremely gifted ballet dancer. Each daughter carved out a niche for herself, avoiding rivalry.

She took her dancing seriously and went on to become one of the best in her country. She loved it from as early as anyone could remember. Aged eleven onwards, she was up at 5.30 a.m. every morning to cross town to attend a special two-hour coaching programme before school. She cannot recall ever having had to give herself 'a kick up the backside' to go and practice, it was just something she adored. She enjoyed being good at it and succeeding in competitions. This is very different from most prodigies, the vast majority of whom have been put under tremendous pressure from parents at a young age.

As Geraldine got older, she moved from winning plaudits at local level, to succeeding at county level, eventually being accepted as one of the best female dancers of her age, nationally. At the main event, aged seventeen, she was rated thirteenth in the country for her particular skills. She knew there were always girls better than she but says, 'I was quite happy with that, there was no chance of my being the very best. Getting there was my claim to fame.' Although she could have gone to a major ballet school and on from there to become a member of the *corps de ballet*, rather than pursuing this any further, she chose to go to university, where she discovered boys and drink. Not that she went wild, just that having devoted herself to dancing in her teens, she felt she needed to relax more, aware that she was a bit shy and lacking in social confidence. University soon put an end to that.

Academically, she limited herself to studying what interested her and to getting good enough grades to keep future options open. Afterwards, realizing she would like a career in dancing, she trained as a teacher and has since set up a studio. To this day she loves the sensation of movement and losing herself in the music, and still dances alone for pleasure. Her studio is thriving, but she does not have grandiose commercial ambitions for it. People often ask if she is going to set up a chain of studios. She explains that all she wants to do is pay off her mortgage and perhaps, ultimately, buy her own professional premises, rather than renting as she does now. Now pregnant by her husband of three years, she expects to go back to work a couple of days a week when the baby is a year old, while an assistant she can rely on runs the studio.

She is unassuming and friendly. That she has a slim figure and a captivatingly pretty face is made incidental by her manner. By being modestly beautiful, rather than overtly, provocatively sexual, she discourages men from relating to her purely as an object of desire, and does not arouse the envy of other women. Her beauty derives partly from the calm, self-confident and considerate impression she creates. She favours tasteful, understated clothing, yet there are some quirky elements to her wardrobe, like her silver cowboy boots and bright orange boiler suits. You feel unthreatened by her, yet she is clearly a determined and capable person. She is lively, chuckling as she recalls her childhood; someone who is not much used to pondering about the past.

She has a wide circle of friends, some from her childhood (she has moved back to the area where she was brought up, close to her parents). However, there are five intimates of whom she says, 'I could call them up and tell them anything at all. If I needed a big favour they would do everything in their power to help me.' Intimacy with such friends is a bedrock of emotional health.

Her father worked his way up to the top of the small company. He was a 'gentle' parent. She has a fond memory of the smell of his hair as she held onto it when he would put her on his shoulders to play pretend horsey games. Her mother, a nurse, was also very affectionate.

Geraldine's devotion to dancing came from enjoyment.

She gave up her career during the period of her daughters' early years and would cuddle them a lot – 'very physical'. Her cousins' mother was less warm, and when they came to play they would get more hugs and cuddles from Geraldine's mum than from their own.

Hers were self-sacrificing parents. During a period when money was short, they became vegetarian so that they could afford to give their daughters meat. They did argue sometimes – Geraldine can remember sitting at the top of the stairs hearing a row – but mostly the relationship was harmonious. Geraldine's husband has commented on how unusually close she is to her father; she is very involved in both parents' lives to this day, and they in hers. Along with her husband's mother, they will help with the childcare when she returns to work.

Asked what ambition her father had for her, she says it was 'to be happy'. Most parents say that, but hers really put it into practice. At school she was never pushed, though she would be restricted to her room if she skived off doing her homework. There was no huge pressure to do well, partly because she always did reasonably well anyway, having no urge to kick against authority. Being a secure, relaxed child, she engaged with the world, and was receptive and able to learn, if she applied herself. She can remember being hit twice by her mother for being naughty, occasions that stand out because they were isolated events. She was not a disobedient or troublesome child, but in any case her parents were not keen on corporal punishment.

Most notable of all, in terms of emotional health, was the fact that she was that very rare thing, an exceptional achiever who had not been driven into it by her parents. Her devotion to dancing came from enjoyment. Her mother did encourage her to go to the studio, but when it was suggested she go every day before school, both parents were a bit doubtful. Although she danced seriously, to a very high level, the fact that it was not a compulsion is shown by the ease with which she gave it up when she went to university. Geraldine is that exceptional person, someone who has remained authentic during both her education and her career.

Geraldine's high-quality early care provided the foundation for her authenticity and aspirations when she went to school and subsequently. As we have seen in the last two chapters, feeling responsively loved as an infant and toddler nurtures identity and fluid, two-way relating. Geraldine did not chase glittering prizes to motivate herself. Rather, she had clear ideas of what she enjoyed and what would be enough success. At school, she could have got top grades if she wanted; she chose not to. She could have been a top ballerina. Today she could expand her business and make much more money, but she prefers to put her family life first. Her early years were the basis for this satiability, but her current emotional health also results from the values her parents passed on to her, and even more important than that, the way in which those values were transmitted.

Identified values

Values are the rules we use to decide what is right and wrong, good and bad, real and true. They get passed down the generations, not by genes, but by patterns of care. For example, parents who steal tend to have offspring who do so too, or who believe stealing is acceptable or even admirable. However, not all children of thieving parents also thieve, and siblings differ in the extent to which they imitate their parents in this and all other respects. It is also the case that plenty of offspring of honest parents are dishonest. So the passing of values from parent to child is not simply a question of imitation or learning, a downloading of moral software – it is also heavily affected by the manner in which parents communicate the values as part of the relationship with the child.

Although conscience has its foundations in identity and emotional security, the way that parents reward and punish their children, from around the age of three, is also tremendously important. By that age children can speak and understand language, with ever-increasing sophistication. Parents' words, as well as the example they set, offer clear indications of what they regard as desirable. If the explicit message is 'it's good to steal', that is going to have an impact. But the key is the response to the child's behaviour. A child whose parent advocates stealing but becomes furious when the child is caught will not be a successful thief. If it's a wily thief you want, much more effective will be to display sympathy and offer tips when the child is caught: 'Bad luck, darling, the next time you go shoplifting it's really important to make sure that there are no security cameras focused on you when you hide the product under your coat.' Of course, most parents are not trying to nurture thieves; my point is that, at its simplest, nothing is more effective in getting a child to adopt your values than the mixture of consistent, pragmatic advice with authentic warmth.

Usually parents encourage offspring to be law-abiding, civil and sociable, and to do well at school. All these goals are infinitely more likely to be achieved if the child actually chooses them for themselves. This is known as 'identification'. The child listens to and watches the parent, and if they are well nurtured, adopts the desired characteristic as an act of will. This volition, deciding to adopt a parental conviction, starts with the parent seeing things from the child's point of view. It is natural for little children to be assertive, demanding even, in their dealings with the world. For instance, to return to stealing, we are not born with a knowledge of property ownership. When placed with other children, the average 18-month-old will try and take a toy from another child eight times per hour. A year later, a toddler will still try to take toys from others three times in the same period. The evolution from this behaviour to a law-abiding citizen depends on how the adults caring for the child react at different ages.

If, early on, the response is angry or forceful, the toddler learns no lessons. It can barely talk or understand what is said to it; explaining a principle like 'it's wrong to take toys from other children' is a waste of breath. However, from around age three, words can be used to help the child see the consequences of grabbing others' toys. For example, the child can be encouraged to think about how it feels when his or her own toys are taken. Then you can ask them how the other child feels when he or she takes *their* toys, fostering a mindfulness of another's experience based on one's own. For much of the time before age five, whilst this kind of reasoning will help, the child will need close watching by a responsive adult, and when it looks as if it is about to do something undesirable, the adult can quickly intervene to forestall atrocities, perhaps gently drawing attention to the principle behind the situation. By around age five, the child should have a pretty good grasp of what is desired, and if the care has been calm and explanatory, and affectionate, it will voluntarily adopt the desired behaviour: identification.

This was clearly the case with Geraldine. Her parents did not impose their values on her, they encouraged her to decide for herself what she did. Whilst they certainly liked the fact that she enjoyed dancing, they were not pulling the strings. A clear sign that identification has occurred is when someone does things throughout life because they enjoy them, like hobbies. At its best, they manage to build a career or find a job based on these interests.

Introjected values

Unfortunately, the kind of care which results in identification is very much the exception. Far commoner is for harassed and exhausted parents to simply bark out more or less angry orders. Of course, all parents are guilty of this sometimes, but in some cases it is continual.

This usually happens from an age when the child is far too young to grasp a principle, and therefore unable to decide voluntarily to do as the parent wishes. The child continues to be 'disobedient', though in reality, before age three, it is merely doing what comes naturally, rather than actually being defiant. Misinterpreting the child's response as wilful and the act of a 'little devil', many parents resort to physical coercion – grabbing toys from the child, for instance – and to actual violence, verbal and physical. Often this is done erratically, the parent becoming furious – letting off steam by shouting and hitting, expressing their emotions rather than trying to teach a lesson.

Too often, the parent is simply unhappy themselves and using the 'disciplining' of the child as a way of expressing their own misery, a dustbin for unwanted emotion. If the parent is angry or sad, creating those emotions in the child can make the parent feel better. The parent's unhappiness might also make them inconsistent in their discipline, so behaviour that was punished last time is liable to be ignored this time, or even worse, rewarded. Frequently the parent engages in 'nattering', keeping up a continual commentary of negative injunctions: 'Don't take that toy, put that toy down, I said put it down, I already told you, put that down.' A vicious circle can arise: the child's behaviour gets ever worse, and this in turn provokes increasingly punitive parental responses.

By age five, the typical child is being more or less coerced into obedience with strict punishments. At one extreme this might mean being made to sit on a 'naughty step' or being sent to their room; at the other, regular beatings. As school rears into sight, middle-class children are particularly likely to find that parental love is conditional on performance. Only if he or she does what the parent wants will he or she be praised and loved. It is true that the combination of coercive early care and this pressure to perform may 'work', in the sense that it results in the child displaying the desired traits. But if so, the child has not *chosen* to be civil or studious, he or she is doing so out of fear of either painful punishment or having love withdrawn. Yes, the child does do his or her homework and says 'please' and 'thank you' on cue. But this is done with a robotic, empty emotion, and not very far beneath the surface, there is usually a sullen, angry sense of menace, while at others a flat, depressed hopelessness. Covert rebellion may ensue. In the teens there is liable to be secret cigarette-smoking, sex and shoplifting.

When parents pass their values on to children in these ways it is known as 'introjection': the child exhibits the principles and desired behaviour but without owning them, instead experiencing them as imposed and meaningless. By contrast, the child who has identified with the values understands why they are doing what they are doing; the introjected child is just going through the motions.

High achievers

A large proportion of exceptional achievers have introjected, rather than identified with, their parents' aspirations. People who identify with values are not compulsive in their quest for success, whereas those who introject are. Plenty of emotionally healthy people could be among the best in their field, like twinkle-toed Geraldine, but they choose not to be. As a rule of thumb, it is safe to say that if you are a high achiever, being emotional healthy is hard, albeit not impossible. Compulsion, resulting from coercive parenting, seems almost essential to get to the top. This is the case with Gloria, the founder and chief executive of a $1-billion company in a Far Eastern country. Ostensibly a glowing tale of rags to riches, hers is really one of sad solitude and emotional ill-health.

When we met I was struck immediately by her demureness. She slunk into the room like a cat, shy and rather British in her desire not to impose on me. In her mid-forties, she had remarkably clear skin and few lines on her face. She reminded me of a bookish 10-year-old,

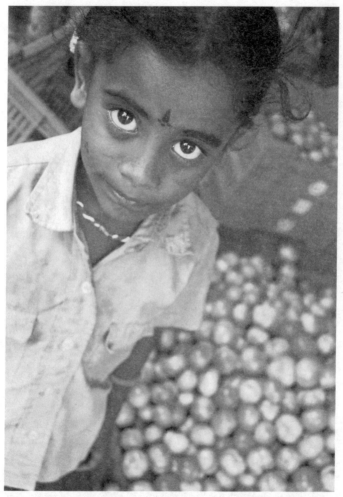
Born in a small village in India, as well as having to apply herself to reading and writing, from the age of eight Gloria had to earn money.

the kind who passes their spare time flitting between Harry Potter and their science homework – sealed off, the sort of girl who is unconcerned about having no friends and has even less interest in boys. Although her clothes looked expensive, I had an impression that she could not care less about them, as if someone had chosen them for her (this turned out to be true – she employs someone to do it). There was a curious feeling of emptiness and invisibility about her, a hologram-like quality.

She was born in a small village in India. Her father died when she was only seven, and because her mother was unable to have any other children, all her mother's aspirations were poured into her. Where she lived there was no running water or electricity; poverty had passed down the generations for millennia. However, her mother was determined that Gloria would be different. Self-improvement was drummed into her from the beginning. She described with a rare display of emotion the fear she felt at failing her mother. A strap would be used to slap the back of her legs if she did less than perfectly at school, or if she showed any sign of independence. Even worse was the coldness. An icy expression on her mother's face accompanied the words, 'So what happened to the other 7 per cent?' when Gloria reported having scored 93 per cent on a maths test.

At the same time, she was constantly required to look after herself and not allowed to depend on her mother. As well as having to apply herself to reading and writing, from the age of eight she had to earn money. She worked in factories and on farms, but she quickly realized she could make more money selling bread and fruit from the market. She found this easy; it was simply a matter of persuading people to make deals with her. She called this 'business', in her mind, and decided early on that it was how she would escape poverty when she was older. One of her teachers told her that 'knowledge is power', and she instantly recognized that education would be the way to succeed in business and became a star student. Aged fifteen, spurred on by her mother, she borrowed the money to go to a big city and slept on the floor of a building where some construction workers from her village were living. She pitched up unannounced at all the best schools to offer herself as a pupil, and finally, after being sent away by most of them, a headmaster allowed her to take a test. She excelled to such a degree that she was immediately accepted. She found a job to pay for the fees and worked eighteen-hour days, mixing schooling with earning. At university she studied biology and afterwards, having spent a few years in a large multinational corporation, identified the product which has subsequently made her a billionaire.

There are a number of textbook features that Gloria shares with others who have introjected values. Losing a parent before the age of fourteen is remarkably common among high achievers. This has been true of 1 in 3 members of every professional domain that has been studied, from British prime ministers to American presidents to British entrepreneurs to French poets. Almost any famous dictator you can think of had this experience. While most people suffering this loss merely find themselves rendered depressed or antisocial by the misfortune, in the case of a small minority, if the prior relationship with the dead parent and the care received after that parent's death are right, the loss seems to inspire a ruthless determination to snatch destiny from fate. In Gloria's case, she had been close to her father and decided at that young age that she must use success to make herself as invulnerable as possible to random chance. Of course it was also vital that her mother coerced her to be a perfect student.

But Gloria has paid a heavy price in her emotional life for this introjection. She has never married or had any sexual relationships. Her mother died when she was in her early twenties and she seems to have suffered a temporary nervous breakdown at that time. Wandering forlorn and confused, she came upon a church and 'took Jesus into my heart'. When I asked if she was happy she said this was not an issue for her. Her face remained impassive; she would not say if she ever felt really down or lonely. She explained that she had Jesus. In fact, as I happened to discover from people who know her well (although they are not close to her, she has occasionally opened up to a few), she lives an isolated, workaholic life, revolving around her employees. She has no truly intimate relationships. Whilst she is enthusiastic about the idea of building her business ever larger, she is someone with no other interests apart from her weekly visits to church.

She is famous for the coldness with which she hires and fires. Despite her anodyne appearance, she is a ruthless businesswoman who has thought nothing of buying and selling companies without heed for the social consequences. The small wages she pays to her compatriots working in the Indian factories where she outsources some of her industrial processes seems not to worry her. She expressed no concern when I raised this.

Success

The coercive methods used by Gloria's mother meant she (Gloria) introjected values, becoming a 'success machine'. When asked, she has no idea why it is important to continually seek to make her company bigger; she has no concept of enough. Although her life might seem like a triumph of the will over adversity, it is nothing of the kind. Gloria was programmed by her mother, and has made very few choices in her life. The death of her father is doubtless a major factor in the scale of her success, making her that much more determined to win in a dog-eat-dog commercial world. But this is not something into which she has any insight; her wish to be successful is a compulsion, driven by the fear of being the victim of fate and another tragic loss.

A great many children of the middle and upper classes in the developed world are subject to similarly coercive care, resulting in introjected values. This is part of the reason why many adults from these classes have been shown to be less aware of the feelings of others, less emotionally intelligent, than adults from less-privileged backgrounds. They are like robots, and often speak of themselves in these terms when they are being really honest. They feel they cannot afford to be concerned with others, they must put themselves first. Having felt neglected and unloved, they have little sympathy for anyone else. At its most extreme this takes the form of subclinical psychopathy, creating a ruthless, cold person, who is manipulative and interested only in advancing their own interests. The vast majority of high achievers come from the higher social classes. That may help to explain why top executives are four times more likely to be subclinical psychopaths.

Of course, how this is expressed must be adapted to the corporation you are working for and the country you live in. There is good evidence that in America disagreeable people end up being paid more than friendly, likeable ones. This finding might seem surprising –

you would have thought that popular people would do best – but in America shoving others out of your way or climbing on their backs is almost essential for success. There is also good evidence that narcissism is rampant among American high achievers. Full-blown narcissism is a state of 'me-me-me' attention-seeking grandiosity. The individual compensates for feelings of worthlessness and invisibility by exhibiting their opposite. One American study measured narcissism in 200 celebrities and in 200 young adults with MBAs. These results were compared with a nationally representative sample using the same questionnaire. Sure enough, the celebs were significantly more narcissistic than both the MBAs and the general population. There were four kinds of celeb included in the sample. The most narcissistic were those who had become famous through a reality-TV show (these individuals also demonstrated high levels of 'exploitativeness' and 'vanity'); next came the comedians (highest on 'exhibitionism' and 'superiority'), then the actors and finally the musicians. Interestingly, the narcissism did not correlate to how long the celeb had been famous, strongly suggesting that fame itself did not make them narcissistic – they were already narcissists beforehand. Young adults with MBAs were chosen for comparison because they were known already to be inclined to narcissism. Sure enough, the MBAs – the business leaders of the future – were significantly more narcissistic than the general population.

The truth is that people who get to the top or into the public eye in America tend to be narcissists. But this is only the tip of their cultural iceberg. The majority of Americans hold unrealistically positive views of themselves, believing they are much better than average in a variety of ways. Indeed, 'bigging yourself up' (known technically as self-enhancement) may be necessary in America. Americans who do so are actually less likely to be mentally ill than those who don't. It may simply be a matter of adaptation to put others down and exaggerate your wonderfulness in such a competitive society. Somewhat bizarrely, researchers characterize those who have realistic appraisals of themselves as suffering from 'depressive realism'.

But this version of social reality is not universal. If you live in Japan and East Asia, far from living in a rose-tinted bubble of positive illusions, if anything you downplay your achievements. In Scandinavia, you cross the road to avoid seeming superior, aiming to level yourself with others. For instance, three times fewer Swedes than Americans (15 per cent versus 46 per cent) estimate themselves to be among the most skillful drivers in their country. This is not to say that citizens of these less self-enhancing nations are cringing pushovers. They do partake in self-enhancement when competing with others from beyond their social networks – business adversaries, for example. Nor do they have diminished individuality. Denmark is ranked the seventh most individualistic country in the world, above most other Western European countries. Yet it also has the strongest tradition of modesty. Denmark, and the rest of Scandinavia, has *Jante* law, which is a system of cultural *mores* that says 'don't think you are better than anybody else'. Although widely derided by Danes as a joke, in practice they adhere to *Jante* law strictly. It is a cultural prototype on a par with its opposite, the American Dream.

A study of Danish and American undergraduates and adults demonstrated that Danes Big It Up considerably less than Americans; in fact, they go to great lengths to play down differences in ability. Yet they are also more independent-minded. For example, the

Danish undergraduates are more likely to think autonomously from their parents' preferences. This reflects parenting and an education system which fosters identification rather than introjection of values.

It is likely that the least emotionally healthy populations are to be found in English-speaking countries like America and Britain – certainly, the prevalence of mental illness among the populations of these countries is twice that of mainland Western Europe, at 23 per cent versus 11.5 per cent. Carving out an emotionally healthy career in such places may be harder. But wherever you live, the key to greater emotional health in your career is to understand the motives and goals you have in the workplace.

Intrinsic and extrinsic goals and motives

Those who, from childhood, identified with their parents' values have what are called 'intrinsic' goals and motives. They do things because they enjoy them. The state of mind during intrinsically motivated activity is a *flow*, a strong connection and oneness with the activity. You become so involved that you forget yourself, and afterwards it seems as if more time has passed than expected. There is a heightened sense of reality and a special freedom.

By contrast, those who have introjected values have what are called 'extrinsic' goals and motives. In choosing a career, and whilst at work, they seek praise and material rewards in order to feel they are fulfilling the aims of parents, and subsequently teachers and employers. *Flow* is fractured by an overriding concern to meet external demands. Focused on the reward, they become disconnected from the pleasures of the activity that produces it. This has been proven many times in experimental studies. When a reward is offered for performing an activity that was initially intrinsically satisfying, there is not only a measurable drop in interest and enjoyment in the individual carrying it out, but also in their motivation to do it at all. For example, in one experiment, two groups of students were given puzzle cubes to play with. One group was paid for doing so, the other was not. The paid ones lost interest sooner and were more likely to stop and read magazines that had been left lying about. Money changed the focus. The unpaid volunteers reported playing with the cube because it was fun or because they chose to; for the paid students, the interesting, enjoyable, challenging aspect of the activity got lost. In the context of work, people with intrinsic motives and goals have been shown to seek intellectual fulfilment, creative self-expression and a sense of mastery in completing tasks. The extrinsic look for evermore money and professional prestige.

Of course, there is an important caveat that must be made about these findings. They do not apply in situations where the person is chasing money or status for reasons of survival. No one has ever been made emotionally or mentally unhealthy by trying to earn enough money to pay for antibiotics that will save their sick child's life, or to buy food for a starving family. *Survival* materialism is the norm for a large slice of the population of the world, who live in absolute poverty, and it does no harm. What is corrosive is *relative* materialism, which only arises in comparatively rich people, like Gloria, who have enough money for food, shelter and medical care, but are trapped on a hedonic treadmill, intent on making more money to fund more luxuries, unable to understand the idea of 'enough', and whose introjected values make them chase evermore success, money and so on.

Exercise

In practical terms, if you are one of these people, there are a number of things you can do to increase your emotional health in terms of your career. Just because you are an employee whose mind and body have been purchased to perform certain tasks by an employer does not preclude intrinsic motivation.

If you write down all the tasks you perform in your job, you will find some promote greater flow than others. Aim to spend more time doing them, if you can. Of course, you may be in a job where there are no opportunities to experience *flow* whatsoever. If so, you need a new career. However, this is rarely necessary. Once you start going with the flow, it's surprising how much more effectively you start doing your work, as well as how much more enjoyable it becomes. This can give you more power and ultimately lead to better pay and greater options.

Office politics

A key part of being emotionally healthy at work is to become adept at office politics (I write about this at greater length in my book *Office Politics*). This skill has been given a bad name. Most people regard it as a nasty device that corporate Machiavellis use to shaft other people

– taking credit for others' work, or passing the blame onto others for their mistakes. In fact, office politics is a normal and unavoidable part of everyday working life. It is inevitable that your interests do not always coincide with those of colleagues or business adversaries, and that in order for you to get what you want, someone else will have to do without. Office politics are what enable this. It requires an awareness of what others are thinking and feeling in the present moment, and of what is in your own mind – both key requirements of emotional health. With this awareness, you can make plans to get your own way, whether that means ensuring a particular job is done well or contributing to the greater good of your organization. (It can, of course, also help you get a raise or the corner office you want.) You also need to learn to 'network', another dirty word. But there is nothing unhealthy about forming alliances with other like-minded people or those whose interests coincide with yours, and cooperating with them. Finally, you need to at least *seem* to be sincere; people must feel you are to be trusted. All of these things are emotionally healthy traits.

It is true that some of the skills required in office politics come more naturally to people who have introjected their values, since who they are has been defined externally from early childhood. 'Chameleonism' is easier if you look outwards for self-definition, for example, and it is true that people who know how and when to be a chameleon are more successful professionally. But that does not mean that those who identified with their parents cannot acquire these skills if they decide to do so, nor does it mean that authenticity need suffer.

To succeed at office politics you need to have certain practical social skills, which does not mean being like this with everyone all of the time. To be a chameleon you have to work out who the other person wants you to be, and then be that person for them.

A manager was having a lot of trouble with one of his bosses. Rather than challenging the boss, he realized that she was someone who spoke in a certain assertive manner and was obsessed by time-keeping. When he adopted a similar manner and – mirroring her – subtly indicated that he was also very concerned to ensure that employees arrived on time, she stopped giving him grief.

To be really good at office politics you need to be able to define precisely what your goal is, devise a plan whereby you can persuade the relevant people to your way of thinking, then choose exactly the right moment to use exactly the right words and manner to express yourself. Elaborate chicanery is almost never required; it is simply a case of understanding how to get what you want, in terms of your self-presentation, your performance. Yes, it helps to be competent at the tasks that the job requires, and to be a hard worker, but without office political skills you will be lucky to thrive. Since the vast majority of jobs in developed nations are in service industries or based in offices, an emotionally healthy person will naturally grasp that knowing how to handle other people – which is not the same as manipulating them in order to exploit them – is essential in order to be effective.

You have to develop authentic personae to survive in the workplace, which sounds like a contradiction in terms. We all develop a variety of personae to deal with others, in all situations, including in family life. At the office, an emotionally healthy person will consciously develop different masks to be put on when dealing with different people. Perhaps you hate one of your bosses. The emotionally healthy person will realize that it's necessary to smile at this boss, sometimes even laugh at their jokes, concealing his or her real feelings.

Of course, in the end, all of us have to spend some of our working hours doing tasks that are not enjoyable. The emotionally healthy person finds ways to spend less time doing such tasks. Using a combination of insight into our motives and greater office political skills, all of us have it in our power to meet the challenge of being more emotionally healthy in our careers. Behind our authentic personae, we can keep our core values intact.

5. Playfulness and Vivacity in Parenting

A father is floating on his back in a swimming pool. His 6-year-old son appears from nowhere and pushes him under the water. The father sinks to the bottom and the boy treads on him. When the father rises to the surface, they laugh uproariously; this is one of their games. The boy also loves to play at punching his father in the stomach as hard as he possibly can, but only when he knows his dad is ready for it. His favourite way of showing affection first thing in the morning is playing 'Jump on Daddy's Tummy'. To outsiders it looks strange, to father and son it is highly amusing.

A mother pretends to go to sleep on the floor, her young daughter does the same several metres away. 'Nighty-nighty,' says the daughter; 'Sleep tight,' replies the mother. After ten seconds the girl says 'Wakey-wakey.' They repeat as necessary.

Most parents can report such exchanges with more or less joy in their voices. The challenge of parenthood is to make it as playful as this for as much of the time as possible. Not only does that foster emotional health in the child, it does so in the parent as well. Two things can stand in our way.

The first – as with everything – is what we bring from our own childhood. Either we repeat our experience, or we react against it. If we had a negative experience, neither tendency is usually conducive

The boy loves to play at punching his father in the stomach as hard as he possibly can . . . To outsiders it looks strange, to father and son it is highly amusing.

to playful, enjoyable parenting. If your own parents were severely punitive it is as unsatisfactory to be equally punitive with your own child as it is to react against your parents' behaviour with unbounded permissiveness. What's needed is for you to metabolize what was done to you, and out of that, to create something new, based on playful enjoyment.

The second obstruction is that many of us could be with the wrong co-parent; the basis on which we have chosen our co-parent is nearly always badly flawed. A compatible, loving partner is not neces- sarily the same an ideal co-parent. As a result, it is not uncommon for parents to find themselves having to deal with the fact that their relationship is a mistake, something I'll discuss in more detail in this chapter. Having first confronted this reality, we must take steps to understand our own situation, out of which playful enjoyment – and from this, emotional health – may emerge.

Motherhood

Whilst becoming a parent is a profound event for both genders, it tends to impact most forcefully on the woman. Motherhood poses the greatest single threat to a woman's mental health. Yet for many it is also the beginning of a dramatic improvement in emotional health.

Over half of British mothers with small babies report feeling in a state of despair. Eighty per cent of those with a child under two say the child has created 'immense strain' in their relationship with their partner, and two thirds say becoming a mother has put them 'completely off sex'. About 10 per cent suffer full-scale postnatal

depression, some of them becoming psychotic (total loss of identity, incoherent confusion). Yet a significant proportion feel far more
emotionally healthy and say that nothing in their life to date has
meant as much to them as becoming a parent. It is a stark example of
the fact that emotional and mental health do not necessarily overlap.

In interviewing over fifty British mothers of under-threes, I met
many who told me that their baby had given them a new lease of life,
and it was the same with fathers. Experiencing the 24-hour dependence of another human being seems to jog us out of our normal
haze of worries about work, money and more or less trivial family
battles. Suddenly those concerns seem petty. We move from the
self-focused state we may have slipped into during the years before
parenthood, to an urgent requirement to concern ourselves with the
needs of another – and this change of focus can be extremely helpful
for emotional health.

Yes, we may be exhausted. Yes, the mother may feel torn between
her desire to pursue a career and the wish to be there for the baby. Yes,
the father may feel anxious about being able to support his family,
and find his eye wandering because his sex life has largely disappeared. Yet both parents often report that until the baby came along
it was as if they and their world had been a fiction. Now everything
starts to feel real again for the first time since their own childhood.

Whether this happens is, of course, hugely influenced by what
happened in childhood. In general, about half of mothers tend to
parent in the same way as their mother, while about half react against
it, although both groups can both imitate and rebel at different times
in their parenting. The arrival of a baby triggers deep memories of
what it meant to be a baby oneself. It activates profound feelings we

have of being neglected or responded to, based on how our carer treated us.

Studies of monkeys as well as humans show the extent to which the way we parent is affected by how we were cared for. Observed across generations, monkey daughters who were lovingly treated by a responsive mother usually treat their own babies in the same way. Animal studies are particularly revealing because it is possible to carry out intergenerational experiments with them, something that is impermissible with humans.

These studies show that the specific amount of care given is duplicated in the next generation. The amount of contact a daughter monkey has with her mother precisely predicts the amount that she bestows on her own daughter, and the same with the granddaughter. Of course, the similarity in mothering across generations could be simply a genetic inheritance – but this has been disproved. The amount of contact the new mother had with her mother has been compared with the average experienced by she her and her sisters. The daughter's subsequent mothering reflects her particular experience, rather than the average for she her and her sisters.

Another theory is that a genetically difficult baby could make the mother uncaring. This was contradicted by a study of what are called highly-reactive infant monkeys, individuals that are very difficult to care for because they overreact to the slightest sound or movement. In a study that would be unethical if undertaken with humans, the monkeys were fostered out to either average mothers or exceptionally nurturing ones. The exceptionally nurtured highly-reactive babies grew up more socially well-adjusted than normal infants fostered by average mothers. Nurture was so influential, in other words, that it could turn

a difficult infant into a superior adult. Furthermore, when the generation of offspring in the study grew up and themselves had infants, their
parenting style, whether exceptionally nurturing or average, precisely
mirrored the kind of care they had received as infants.

What goes for monkeys does not always go for humans. In this
case, it does so only up to a point. In general, it is true that studies of
humans show that parents who had good early care tend to provide
it themselves, and vice versa. However, where humans differ is
that they have language, and this gives them the capacity for self-
consciousness, which in turn creates the possibility of volition. Some
mothers reflect on their own experience and decide to act differently
themselves, something a monkey cannot do.

For example, from early infancy, Gillian, a 52-year-old journalist,
was left by her mother to scream. Her mother was firmly of the view
that babies need to be 'shown who is boss'. If you gave in to them,
the 'little rascals would twist you round their little fingers'. The result
was a nervy, mildly depressed Gillian, who became a jumpy adult.
However, when motherhood came along, she suddenly underwent
a big change. She became confident, calm and assured, absolutely
determined at all costs not to repeat her mother's mistakes. A monkey
cannot decide to act differently from its mother, but a human can.
Gillian tuned into each of her three offspring, careful to leave several
years between each in order to do so, and succeeded in giving them a
very solid start. Playful enjoyment abounded in the succeeding years.
Alas, it is not always so simple. If only we humans merely needed to
decide to be different in order to do so.

Like Gillian's mother, Julia's was coldly neglectful. Additionally,
she was only able to see Julia as a vehicle for her own unfulfilled

Exceptionally nurtured highly-reactive baby monkeys grew up more socially well-adjusted.

aspirations. A stellar career as a corporate lawyer resulted. Julia also enjoyed sexual relationships with a long succession of men, tending to want her independence and reluctant to settle down. Finding herself in her late thirties, she decided to have children and got together with a rather glamorous younger man. But when babies arrived, she found herself torn into pieces by conflicting desires, of which the strongest was to give her children the love she never had. However, her addiction to career success made this hard to achieve. She found it impossible to stay at home and care for the children because she needed the antidepressant effect of daily workplace status and battles. Yet she also found it impossible to employ adequate substitute care. Even though she could afford a nanny, somehow the ones she picked were always lacking in the responsiveness and empathy essential for babies and toddlers. Ironically, the nannies she chose ended up giving her children the same experience of neglect that her mother had provided. Never having been loved herself, she did not have enough insight – a key element of emotional health – to recognize those nannies who would be different from her mother. She imagined a good nanny would be one who was going to be 'educative' and 'efficient', whereas love matters far more. There was precious little space for play and enjoyment for anyone.

The story illustrates that it is not always enough to *decide* to give your children a different experience; you may find it hard to put your wishes into practice because you have competing impulses. A crucial issue is which branches a woman has been following prior to motherhood, in terms of her attitude to her femininity, career and maternal identity.

In Britain, the studies of psychologist and psychoanalyst Joan Raphael-Leff reveal that women have three main patterns of response to a baby. The *Hugger* is filled with prenatal fantasies of what the baby will be like when it is born, and subsequently sees it as her job to adapt to the baby. She may sleep with it in the bed, will want to breastfeed for as long as possible, and adores the snuggly feeling of living in a little bubble with her newborn, often staying in bed with it for the first week. She is the least likely kind of mother to return to work while the child is under three. The *Organizer* is the opposite. She has had few or no thoughts about what kind of person the foetus is, and after the birth, sees it as her job to help the uncivilized creature acquire independence and to learn how to fit into the needs of the family as soon as possible. She imposes routines in the name of helping the baby to sleep and eat at times which fit into *her* life. She is much more likely to return to work, often finding the baby dull company. In Britain these two groups each represent about a quarter of mothers (in other nations the proportions differ; in America, for example, Organizers are more common). The remaining half of British mothers are *Fleximums*, a mixture of the other two kinds. The Fleximum may adopt some routines, whilst also adapting to the baby's wishes in other respects. She is aiming for a win–win situation, a pattern which will enable both She and the baby to feel content. Part-time work may appeal, especially if it can be done from home.

None of these groups is likely to be more emotionally healthy than the others, for each approach can have its problems. The commonest is if the woman is forced by circumstances, or by impulses arising from her relationship with her mother, to adopt patterns which feel wrong. For example, the emotional health of a Hugger suffers if financial pressures require her to work full-time. If an Organizer tries to act like a Hugger (perhaps reacting against her mother) but cannot enjoy being 'stuck' at home, she may become depressed. A Fleximum who tries to please everyone but ends up pleasing no one is not going to enjoy emotional health. What is vital is that each woman interrogates her history and present feelings, and uses that knowledge to create the right regime for her and her baby.

Insight and playfulness

Serena was always a studious girl, who enjoyed her time at school. Her mother provided stable, affectionate care and her father was an impressive achiever. However, she felt shocked and let down by him when he went off with a younger woman when she was seventeen. Having been told that she had to put work before boys she was furious at his hypocrisy, and decided it was time to let rip, embarking on a wild affair with a sexy older man. This did not stop her from getting to a top university and into a highly paid job in financial services. Although she enjoyed herself to the full during her twenties in a series of exciting relationships, in her early thirties she was quite deliberate in her choice of husband. With cold calculation, she recognized that her sexual allure would decline as she got older, and she married. She was also aware that the odds of any child she had being born with abnormalities – and of not being able to conceive a child at all – rise rapidly after the mid thirties. The man she chose was not a philanderer, he was a cerebral high-achiever in her field. She admired and loved him but was not 'in love' with him; he was nowhere near as sexy as some of her previous lovers. As the babies came, she was clever enough to identify a niche in her field, which allowed her to work part time. The nanny she employed to substitute for her when she was not there was also wisely chosen: she told me she did not want one who would be constantly taking her children to meet others, or would seek to 'educate' and 'stimulate' them. She had grasped that all small children need is the constant attention of a loving and responsive adult (and this person does not have to be a biological parent). The outcome is playful, jolly children and a playful, jolly Serena.

Another triumphant example of a mother who was insightful enough to avoid repeating her past is Penny. She lives in the present, alert to what is happening here and now. At school, she never cared how well she did and, although she passed few exams, she does not see herself as in any way inferior to her more highly qualified peers. She was someone who always wanted to be a mother, and 'did jobs' until that point, rather than having a career. Tremendous adversities accompanied motherhood. She had twins, putting enormous pressure on her (unsurprisingly, mothers of twins are at higher risk of depression). She suffered a serious physical illness during their early years, and again when she went on to have two more children. Her husband provided minimal support, heading off to work before the children were up, and returning only after they were asleep. Yet none of this mattered. Although a Hugger by inclination, Penny was forced by circumstances to be a Fleximum in the way she cared for her children.

Her emotional health had its roots in a rock-solid relationship with both her mother and her grandmother. They supported her throughout her travails. Her father had been a drunken scoundrel who left her mother when she was small, but to everyone's surprise he became a tremendously playful and buoyant figure for his grand-children, providing fun and games and indulgence that Penny was often too overstretched to offer. Critical was her capacity for insight, the element of emotional health I explored in Chapter One. She is not an intellectual person, given neither to theorizing nor to intro-spective navel-gazing. Yet she worked out that she needed to avoid repeating her mother's mistakes in her choice of partner. During her teens and twenties she had relationships with a series of lovable rogues. There came a point when she realized that she was merely repeating her mother's mistakes, and very deliberately sought out someone who, though less glamorous, arousing and wealthy than some of her other suitors, was reliable. Whereas her mother had led a louche and permissive sexual life, Penny decided to avoid that. This brings us to the second main challenge of parenting: learning to make the best of the bad job that is the average couple.

Your co-parent

Unlike Penny, nearly all of us choose our co-parent using incorrect criteria. On first meeting, it is extremely rare that either party gives serious consideration to whether the other is the right person with whom to embark on the project of having children. Nearly always, we originally choose our mate on the basis of sexual desire and status. In a rational world, these criteria would never be primary.

Of course, for a baby to result, both parties do need to want to have sex with the other. But the fact that a woman wears a short skirt of a particular cut and fabric, which reveals legs of a particular thickness and texture, and that these factors in turn appeal to specific desires in a man that go back to his childhood, is hardly the basis for deciding whether she is going to do a good job of collaborating as a parent. Likewise, the fact that a man made you laugh or that you noticed he had nice hands or a pleasing bum when you first met, is not a basis for shared parenthood. Equally unhelpful is the extent to which we are influenced by the prospective partner's wealth or success or popularity. It would be unwise to select your car primarily on the basis of its colour, or your career because of the kind of clothing it requires. What someone looks like, or their superficial charm, is not the basis for finding the right person for cooperating in the care of children. The challenge is for both partners to accept that they have made this mistake and find ways to make it fruitful.

A critical distortion is the extent to which we have been influenced in this choice by the traits of our opposite-sexed parent. The first proof of this came from a cunning study done in 1980 in Hawaii, where there are many mixed-race marriages. A thousand men and women were identified who came from mixed parentage. In two thirds of cases, their first marriage had been to a partner of the same ethnic origin as their opposite-sexed parent. In two thirds of cases a woman married a man of the same skin-colour as her father, likewise sons with their mothers and wives. The particularly clever aspect of this study is that all the sample had divorced and remarried. Sure enough, in two thirds of cases their second partners were also of the same ethnicity as the opposite-sexed parent. This is powerful evidence that how our mum or dad looks determines our choice of who we shack up with (and, perhaps, also that we do not learn from our mistakes).

Romauld et Juliette (1989): These characters are the exception, but studies show that we are more likely to pick partners with the same appearance of our opposite-sexed parent.

Subsequent studies have revealed that we are more likely to pick partners with the hair- and eye-colour of our opposite-sexed parent, likewise when it comes to their smell. But it also extends to whether or not we were emotionally close to that parent. Sure enough, both women and men who were close to their opposite-sexed parent are even more likely to choose mates who resemble them. A particularly telling study used a sample of adopted girls. Only if they had been close to their adoptive dad did they end up married to a man who looked like him. This proved it was all about nurture, and could have nothing to do with nature. In another study, of forty-nine women, the precise dimensions of their fathers' faces were mapped out scientifically (distance between eyes, size of nose and so on). The women were then shown pictures of fifteen men's faces and asked to select the one they found most attractive. If they had a positive relationship with their dad, they were significantly more likely to pick out the face which resembled his in its dimensions.

The fact that the past is such a huge influence makes it likely that you select someone as a co-parent who you would not have chosen if approaching the matter rationally. For those who had emotionally healthy opposite-sexed parents it works fine, but for most of us that was not the case, and therefore the consequent dilemma is stark: stick it out with this person, or split up and move on.

As already described in Chapter Three, the evidence shows that not only is separation usually very harmful to children, it is all too often of no benefit to the adults either. In most cases, it is much better for each partner to do their best to sort themselves out, rather than imagining that the grass will be greener in another field. Without insight, the odds are that you will merely repeat the same mistake again in your choice of the next partner, resulting in another break-up. Only when you have dug very deep inside yourself should you conclude that the madness or badness of your partner is grounds for a separation. Of course, such cases do exist.

Caroline is a 45-year-old mother whose parents divorced when she was small, following her father's infidelities. She is still in touch with this moody, tyrannical man, but has come to accept that he will never be a half-decent father to her. Luckily, her mother was loving and quietly supportive, and Caroline did well in her education and subsequently in her career. She married an ambitious, successful businessman, whom she believed would offer the security that her father had not, and she herself gave up work to care for their children. Living in a world of rich corporate executives, she was increasingly regarded as an adjunct to her husband. The lives of these executives revolved around huge expenditure on possessions and holidays, while the wives used conspicuous consumption as the marker of their status. She felt desperately lonely: her husband no longer took her seriously, and she was very bored. For a time she dealt with this by joining a religious cult, which stole some of their money. At the same time, she discovered that her husband had been visiting prostitutes throughout their married life, and that this was the norm among his peers. On discovering this, as she put it to me,

> something in me snapped, or woke up. What the hell was I doing with this revolting person? How had I let myself drift so far from what I cared about? I had to get out. It took me three more years to pluck up the courage to leave. I knew that leaving is incredibly painful, rarely the right thing. It was

a nightmare process emotionally, but I am still glad I did. I have all but disinfected myself of the world that had such a grip on me. I met and married my old school sweetheart, who was entirely unlike my first husband. My children and I are so happy, so carefree now. We laugh and love so much.

Crucial for this happy ending was Caroline's ability to understand how her own childhood had caused her to pick her first husband, and that she did not just leap out of the proverbial frying pan into another marital fire. Instead of simply deeming her husband mad or bad, she paused for three years, looked into herself and by doing so was able to make a good decision when it came to seeking a new partner.

How to generate playfulness in parenting

As we have seen, parenting poses two main challenges. The first is understanding how our reactions to our children are a response to how we were cared for. Only when this is clear to us can we do something about it – and unlike monkeys, we do have that option. The second challenge is to admit the extent to which we might have made a mistake in our choice of co-parent: almost everyone does. Having admitted this, instead of blaming everything on the other parent, you have to accept that a mistake has been made and start making the best of it (or, if really necessary, start again with someone else, as Caroline did). That also means carefully observing any tendency to wrongly identify the traits of your parents in your partner, at the same time as acknowledging the ways in which your partner *is* a duplicate of your opposite-sexed parent. Having done so, you can begin to carve out a relationship based on what the two of you are really like, and find ways in which you can enjoy each other, generating playfulness in your parenting, getting on the same side, and fostering mutual emotional health. A marital therapist who really understands this – perhaps with a background in what is known as transactional psychology (see the Transpersonal Therapy website) – can be very helpful. This newfound way of looking at your co-parent can become a platform for enjoying parenthood and offering your own children a pleasing model for their lives.

Parents may be reading this book with an increasingly heavy heart, because they are aware that the care they have provided has created problems for their offspring. If so, do not despair. If you have a child with problems (aged three years to puberty) – problems that might be as insignificant as shyness, or as big as continual gloominess – there is a simple method I have developed for resetting the child's emotional thermostat, called *Love Bombing*. This involves arranging focused, one-to-one time with your child, perhaps on a weekend away, to develop playfulness, vivacity and love – I have given more detail in the Homework section.

That we repeat the past is inevitable. But never forget that some of that repetition is hugely beneficial to our emotional health. For instance, mothers who are loved become loving mothers themselves. Whilst it is true that we do, inevitably, mess our children up to some degree, that is not the whole story.

Conclusion:
Meeting the Challenges

What is the purpose of our existence? Perhaps it is simply to be machines that propagate our selfish genes. Some say it is to be pious vehicles of God's will. Others that there is no reason; life is purposeless. I believe the reason is in order to improve our emotional health: to be living more in the present, more authentically and insightfully; to have more fluid, open relationships with others; and to be more playful and vivacious. But how can we meet the challenges to improvement?

Because success can only ever be partial, it helps not to set the hurdle too high. Focussing on happiness as a goal is destructive: it is unattainable. The same goes for mental health: there are no completely mentally healthy people. *Improved* emotional health is much more realistic. Nobody reaches the top of the tree of emotional health, but you can hope to achieve incremental small steps along your branch. These little movements will gradually take you back to the trunk and upwards; in terms of emotional health, that is good enough.

You do, however, need to know which branch you are on to start with – it is hard to go forwards until you know which way you're facing. But even more important is understanding *why* you are on this particular branch. Finding ways to change how your childhood is impacting negatively on you today is crucial.

How did you get here?

A 58-year-old man wrote to me as follows:

> I was rejected by my 25-year-old mother in the early weeks
> after an emergency caesarean and then treated as 'an object'
> by her for two or three years after that – a tool for her use.
> My particular 'way in' to this self-knowledge came via the
> discovery of the 'shame' that had lain undetected within
> me for many, many years. Now that I have uncovered it, the
> shame of not being loved is slowly fading, but it is a hard nut
> to crack and my task has not been made easier by the general
> ignorance of it amongst therapists and counsellors, and how
> to 'treat' it.

Here is a man who has accepted that there are no shamans, no
wizards, no idealized experts who can provide him with The Answer,
but who is working hard to use what help can be provided. If you do
go to a therapist, or a priest or the like, do not let the fact that they
often get things wrong worry you. Of course, if they are nearly always
wrong, and fail to 'get' you, you should have no compunction about
going elsewhere, but if they are even partly helpful, then fine – you
must not expect too much.

The man went on to write:

> Not long after my son was born twenty years ago, when my
> mother was in her late fifties, she visited us. During a discus-
> sion, quite loudly and openly, she said of my young son:

'Isn't it nice to have a toy to play with?' My wife and I were speechless. That remark shows both the extent of the child-hood 'neglect' by her own parents and her complete lack of self-awareness.

But sadness and rage towards a parent can be followed by forgiveness and understanding. The man concluded:

It took me forty-five years or so to work out (with the help of your books and some others) what had happened and what effect it had had on me, and by the time my mother died some ten years later I had managed to talk to her about it on a few occasions. While never actually admitting to what had happened, she never denied it either. Her attitude, which I actually learnt to respect her for, was to say: 'If the things you say happened, happened, then I am sorry. I meant you no harm.' One of the lessons that I have learnt is not to take the 'abuse' too personally, the fact is that she would have done (or failed to do) everything she did to any son who had been born to her at that time. So, 'nothing personal'!

Take stock of what you have

Another place to start your journey is with an appreciation of what you have, as well as what is lacking. There is nearly always good as well as bad in what our parents provided. What is more, the vast majority of people living in developed nations simply have no idea how lucky they are. Unlike much of the rest of the population of the world, we have sufficient food, electricity, healthcare, education, and freedom to do pretty much what we want – with the aid of any number of devices we take completely for granted (mobile phones, cars, computers and the internet). If only we could be satisfied with what we have got, materially, we could start to focus on the other stuff, which is so integral to emotional health: our intimates, our friends, our communities and hobbies, as well as more profound experiences, like enjoyment of the arts, or spending time in beautiful natural places, or spiritual pursuits – in fact, whatever rocks your inner boat.

Sleepwalking through life is not a new problem. Perhaps its most powerful literary evocation is Leo Tolstoy's short story *The Death Of Ivan Ilyich*. A judge in the Russian ruling elite, he discovers he has cancer. With exquisite skill, Tolstoy takes Illytch on a journey back through his life. Agonizing honesty makes him realize that it has been a futile farce. As he faces the bankruptcy of his relationships and aspirations, he feels nothing but horror at his wife's shallow concerns and pretensions; even his children seem distant and pointless. His friends have no real empathy with him. He has achieved nothing of worth in his career, having been a mere functionary in a corrupt and exploitative ruling class. It might sound as if he has simply developed a clinical depression, but in fact, through making this journey, he achieves a rebirth on his deathbed.

A significant proportion of emotionally healthy people have been through a similar journey. It seems to take something as extreme as the threat of actual death – or at least social death – to wake many people up. It can happen at almost any age. A woman in her early thirties had had a mother who was given to wild ideas, frequently deciding on the spur of the moment to set off in their car around America, a chaotic itinerant. The mother was frequently quite crazy; as a 5-year-old, the woman had often had to be the adult just in order to make sure they survived. Whilst her childhood left her feeling insecure, it also meant that, however much money she earned, she always appreciated having enough food in her cupboard. Even today, she keeps it well stocked and gains succour from the thought that she will not starve. With the help of a considerate and loyal family friend, and subsequently a good therapist, she turned into an impressively emotionally healthy person.

Another example is that of the workaholic man who noticed that his wife seemed to be spending a remarkable amount of time hanging out with his best friend. Asked if they were having an affair, she denied it. Two years passed before he realized that they were indeed having an affair, and a divorce followed. So did a nervous breakdown. He told me, 'I went to the bottom of the hole, I'd had it. I felt dreadful, certainly suicide crossed my mind.' However, in the contemplation of his end came a beginning. With the help of a counsellor, he reappraised his whole life. 'A lot of people are just grinding their lives out. It was only because I got to the bottom of the hole that I started to climb my way out.' He saw his counsellor weekly for a few months and she encouraged him to read a book on meditation. Using that book, rather than through any direct teaching, he developed a daily meditation routine, which could also be employed at any time he felt distressed. Today he is an alive person, with a sparkle in his eyes, always doing his best to be alert to what is going on around him socially and psychologically, a vibrant presence. Practices such as meditation, which increase mindfulness of our moment-to-moment feelings, thoughts and bodily states, as well as those of others, can be a huge help in shifting us out of our tendency to live second-hand, at one remove from the present.

Is a catastrophe such as the breakdown of a marriage or the threat of death the only way to become emotionally healthy? For some of us that may be so. Some people are so far along the lower branches of the tree of emotional health that it will take an event of this kind of severity in order to move them upwards. But for most of us it does not have to be so extreme. There are innumerable ways that we can make a more gradual shift. Hopefully, reading this book, and thinking about the subjects it discusses – insightfulness; sense of self; fluid, two-way relationships; authenticity; and playfulness and vivacity in your life – will have got you started.

To build on this, you can perform a simple exercise.

Exercise

Write down all the aspects of your life which you feel deplete you. These may be negative traits like being bad-tempered or lazy or feckless, but also, perhaps, things that you feel you do not appreciate enough – your partner, say, or your children. Now you need to find a place that you can think of as your symbolic grave. It could be a quiet corner of a field, if you live in the countryside; or perhaps somewhere in your garden, if you have one. Or it could just be a place in your house, like a floor in a peaceful room. Now lie down in that 'grave' and imagine the worst possible scenario.

Picture yourself as having died, looking up from the grave in which you have been lain, and imagine that you have completely squandered your life, wasting your talents and all the goodwill that those who love you offered. Looking down on you are all the significant people in your life, from partners to children to parents to friends to valued teachers to colleagues. Now imagine that they are expressing all their fury and resentment at the terrible waste that your life has been. They feel not a shred of pity or regret at your death, only outrage at your foolish failure to make the most of what was there. Listen to their voices, picture them screaming and shouting at your dead body, as you lie there. Imagine precisely what they would be saying. Your child might be shouting, 'How could you have spent so much time working when you could have been playing with me?', your partner might be saying, 'You would never let me know what you were thinking; it's too late now, you fool!', your valued teacher might be berating you for 'all that wonderful skill you had in writing essays, squandered by dissipating drink and drugs'.

Only when they have given full vent to this frustration should you let the sound die down. In its place, start to picture the vows you will make to yourself to do the things that will prevent it being like that when you truly die. Write down at least five things, and every morning for the next month, before you start your day, read through them and vow to live by them: promise to start loving yourself, attending to others, and all the other things that most of us fail to do.

Picture yourself in a place that you can think of as your symbolic grave. It could be a quiet corner of a field if you live in the countryside.

Beyond this book

Of course, simply reading this book and doing an exercise may not be enough. Alas, merely willing oneself to be different does not take account of the extent to which our customary patterns are ingrained as an established, habitual set of brainwaves and chemicals. To deal with that, it is unavoidable that you retrace the steps along the branches that led you to this place. There are a host of ways of doing this. There are countless self-help books that provide invaluable opportunities for people to examine their emotional history. Many novels are also tremendously helpful and I have suggested some further reading in the Homework section that follows. Indeed, books can occasionally be a sufficient revelation on their own – although for people who are prone to intellectualizing their problems, reading can merely be a cerebral escape, which does not convert into actual changes in behaviour or quality of experience.

For others, there is no doubt that spiritual practices are enormously helpful. As I mentioned earlier, people who have a weekly observance are significantly less likely to be mentally ill than those who do not. That does not necessarily mean they are emotionally healthier, but it can be the case. It does not matter which religious or spiritual practice or ethical code you follow, what seems to be important is that you have one. In the case of alcohol or drug abuse, for example, there is a practical level at which organized religion can help teenagers. Quite simply, if their religion prohibits use, and they are devout, they are not at risk. That does not mean they will be emotionally healthy; indeed, religious devotion can leave people feeling very inhibited and oppressed. But refraining from substance abuse increases the chances of mental health. By implication, you can see that having a particular code of ethics could help you to avoid making self-destructive choices when it comes to hedonism, for instance (having affairs or compulsive gambling, for example). Nor should one scoff at good habits such as a healthy diet, regular exercise and ensuring sufficient sleep. Accompanied by relaxation techniques like yoga and meditation, some people can use these habits as building blocks for a better life.

All of which begins to equate emotional health with a Spartan goody-goody-ness. Of course that is mistaken. There is nothing wrong in itself with excess, with the enjoyment of bodily pleasures – be they food, sex or chemically induced moods and sensations. The problem arises only when these pleasures become compulsive. So long as volition is operating, almost anything goes. There is no moral code shared by all emotionally healthy people, the key thing, as I have said, is that they have a set of values with which they regulate themselves, based not on what parents and society insist is right, but rather their own experience.

Serious help

For some, professional help may be what's needed. This could include short periods of taking medicines like antidepressants. If you choose to go down this route, you should never forget that antidepressants have side-effects (such as reduced libido) and undesirable effects on your psyche (such as a blunted response to beauty). Furthermore, the great majority of the effect these medicines have is achieved by

Good habits such as a healthy diet and regular exercise, accompanied by relaxation techniques like yoga and meditation, can be the building blocks for a better life.

the individual's *wish* that they will have the desired effect, known as a placebo effect. Not that this means antidepressants should be dismissed; so long as they reduce your depression, then they are valuable as a short-term expedient. But in most cases you should not need to take them for more than six months at a time.

There are also non-chemical temporary reliefs, like Cognitive Behavioural Therapy (CBT), which may help to keep you from falling off the tree altogether. These treatments entail using thoughts to control feeling, a sort of hypnotism. By constantly challenging your negative thoughts and offering more positive ones instead, you may be able to gain a fragile and superficial optimism. That is better than nothing.

Where drugs and the likes of CBT can be immensely damaging is the tendency of some proponents to explicitly prohibit patients from looking back to the childhood, where the problems began. Those prescribing the drugs may tell you that your problem is caused by genes. I don't believe they are deliberately lying when they tell you this, merely that they are not yet aware of the powerful evidence from the Human Genome Project, which shows that this is simply not true in the vast majority of cases. In order for emotional health to happen, the early years must be understood, and the lead of maltreatment converted into the gold of insight.

The most obvious way of achieving this is to seek out therapies that focus on the past. There are short-term methods which can make a huge difference:

• For depressed people, the *Hoffman Process* is a week-long residential dive into your childhood, and can be a revelation. It is often not sufficient on its own, but it can be an excellent place to start.

- Likewise, sixteen sessions of Cognitive Analytic Therapy take you through your early years before using that knowledge to address a specific problem, such as a tendency to chase the wrong sort of partner, or falling out with your boss.
- Group therapies can help with specific problems, like addictions and shyness.
- Transactional Analysis (or Transpersonal Therapy) can be enormously rewarding, taking you back to childhood and offering rich redemption.

Beyond that, there is the more intensive and long-term help provided by psychoanalytic therapists. In this case, much depends on the personality and emotional health of the therapist, which are perhaps even more important considerations than the theories that govern their work. Whatever kind of therapy you pursue, you do need a therapist who explicitly agrees, at the outset, that the task is to understand how your past exists in the present. If you go to someone who professes to represent any of the schools listed above, you should challenge them at the outset to demonstrate this clearly, and if they provide ambiguous answers, you should look elsewhere. You should listen to your initial feelings in picking a therapist. If the person just does not seem very warm or intelligent, or right for you, you need someone else.

In the end, there is no ideology which will result in improved emotional health, be it religious, philosophical, psychological, medical or, for that matter, political. Emotional health is every individual's daily challenge. As I have indicated, there is no point at which a human being solves the problem: 'Sorted – now I'm emotionally healthy'. Complete emotional health is a state that we can only strive towards.

My mother was a fine example of this. She had a difficult childhood, to say the least. Her mother was a cold woman and my mother was cared for by a nanny, a woman who was effectively her mother, but who – despite being loving – was also often harsh, hitting my mother. My mother's father committed suicide when she was fourteen, her favourite brother was homosexual and also killed himself, shortly before the birth of the second of her four children. She found caring for us a struggle – not surprising, given that at one point there were four of us under five. In middle age, and before the death of my father, I would say that she was never very contented, although she often displayed some emotionally healthy features, like vivacity and playfulness. However, after the death of my father, she lived a further ten years and blossomed. Her tendency towards depression receded. She became a good listener, judicious in her suggestions, lively and engaged. She was more than dutiful to her friends, yet never sentimentalized her relations with them. I would say she was emotionally healthy, in many respects and for much of the time in this last period of her life.

Improved emotional health is open to all of us, all of the time. True, there are many challenges, perhaps the greatest of which is the position our childhood leads us to occupy on the tree of emotional health. But with goodwill – and always remembering my mother's motto: 'hope for the best, expect the worst' – we can, with insight, carve out healthier relationships and more authentic, vivacious, playful and first-hand living.

Homework

The following section includes works that have been valuable sources in the writing of this book, and also additional ideas to help you understand emotional health. They are all recommended further reading.

Introduction: Are You Emotionally Healthy?

Leo Tolstoy's short story *The Death of Ivan Ilyich* is a brilliant evocation of the importance of waking up and smelling the coffee, for those of us living in affluent societies. A conventionally successful member of the Russian ruling elite discovers he has cancer. By the time he is on his death-bed he realizes that his life has been spent in empty social exchanges and that he feels no authentic intimacy with any of his family members. His epiphany challenges what it means to be normal or sane or happy, and offers the potential for something more profound.

Erich Fromm's book *To Have or To Be* is a view of emotional health that is anchored in his Buddhist, psychoanalytic Marxism. A member of the Frankfurt School of psychoanalysis, Fromm shows how both one's childhood history and modern capitalism can prevent us from understanding what really matters in life. He offers an alternative to conventional existence.

Mike Leigh's 2008 film *Happy-Go-Lucky* portrays a young woman whose emotional health seeps out into the life of those around her.

Listen to Gary Jules's version of the song 'Mad World'. Its sadness at how dead too many people feel is heartbreaking, and can be a launchpad for seeking a better way.

1. Insightfulness

Edward St Aubyn's five Melrose books, *Never Mind, Bad News, Some Hope, Mother's Milk* and *At Last* (Picador), are about the life of a man who was sexually abused by his father as a child and neglected by his mother. Struggling with drug addiction and unstable relationships, the central character battles to carve out some capacity for choice in his life, as he overcomes the legacy of his difficult childhood. It offers a realistic picture of what redemption might consist of.

Many people have written to me saying that they found my book, *They F*** You Up – How To Survive Family Life* (Bloomsbury 2006), very helpful in making sense of how different components of their childhood history have affected their adult personality. Linda Hopkins's biography of the psychoanalyst Masud Khan, *False Self* (Other Press, 2006), describes a man who fought to have insight into his flawed character and who failed. Using the journal Khan kept of his secret thoughts and feelings, she shows how he struggled to cope with his sense of powerlessness and insignificance. Oddly enough, in his failure to achieve insight there is a hope for all of us – it is not easy to make sense of your past and to really change how you behave in the present, but just because Khan failed does not mean we cannot succeed. Hopkins suggests some of the ways in which insight can elude us. The book also provides an interesting account of how the psychoanalytic movement developed between the 1950s and the 1980s.

Alfred Hitchcock's 1945 film *Spellbound* beautifully, as well as entertainingly, shows how careful exploration of one's past – in this case using a dream (including sets designed by Salvador Dali) – can help a person to alter their behaviour in the present, based on understanding how childhood trauma is being enacted.

John Lennon's song 'Mother' is a plaintive cry to his mother for leaving him. It can be found on the album *John Lennon / Plastic Ono Band*, which includes several other moving songs about the impact of his childhood on him. Another song, *You Choose*, on the Pet Shop Boys album *Release* is an amusing attempt to encourage the listener to accept responsibility for a state of mind which we usually assume is beyond our control: falling in love.

2. Living in the Present: A Sense of Self

Almost anything written by P. G. Wodehouse – but especially the Wooster stories – has vibrant characters who live in the present, and that vibrancy can rub off on the reader. Although thought of as a children's book, *Peter Pan* by J. M. Barrie also powerfully conveys what it feels like to be in the present – few fictional characters do so more than Peter Pan himself. The novel *Engleby* (Vintage, 2008), by Sebastian Faulks, subtly explores the multiple personae that a seemingly quite normal person might have. It also conveys the problems of living at second hand.

Mark Williams's book on *Mindfulness* (Piatkus, 2011) offers a guide to how to get in touch with the present moment, and a CD which can be used as a practical aid.

The BBC adaptation of John le Carré's veiled autobiography, *A Perfect Spy* (available on DVD), provides a well-observed analysis of why we develop secret lives. The book on which the series is based is equally good.

It's impossible to choose a song that makes everyone feel alive, since it so depends on personal taste. 'Dynamite' by Taio Cruz would blast my 7-year-old son into the present – not that he lives anywhere else for most of the time (he is now eight and has moved on to 'All Along The Watchtower' by Jimi Hendrix). More contemplative might be 'I Know That My Redeemer Liveth' from Handel's *Messiah*. For me, it's the whole second side of the Beatles album *Abbey Road*, but especially 'Golden Slumbers'.

3. Fluid, Two-Way Relationships

Being fluid and two-way in relationships does not mean spilling your guts; it can be very subtle, as is evident in the cunning and perceptiveness displayed by Jane Austen when she describes her characters' complex and often implicit communications. All of her books are superbly written, but many people feel *Emma* is the most remarkable. The books offer an ethical map for conducting oneself in dealing with our fellow humans. Equally edifying, in a different way, is my favourite Evelyn Waugh book, *A Handful of Dust*. Its account of a husband's betrayal by his wife is chilling. Perhaps most powerful of all is T. S. Eliot's poem 'The Love Song of J. Alfred Prufrock'. It conveys the loneliness of the single person, although happily for Eliot he found love in his later years and largely gave up writing such searingly honest and deep poems.

There are no simple solutions to marital discord, but the best self-help method is called Imago Therapy. In essence, it entails repeating back to your partner what he or she says, and checking that you have understood them correctly. Harville Hendrix is the author of *Getting the Love You Want* (Pocket Books, 2005), the clearest popular account of the method. Approaching relationships from a different angle, *Solitude* by Anthony Storr (Simon & Schuster, 2005) persuasively contends that we place too high a value on relationships in modern life, demanding too much of them. He maintains that there is much to be gained from our own company.

Perhaps the greatest television drama ever made, Dennis Potter's *Pennies From Heaven* (BBC, available on DVD) explores relationships and the differences between the genders. Using popular classics from the 1930s, the characters occasionally break into song to convey their inner states, mouthing the words as if in a musical. Leaving aside the fact that this was the most innovative and imaginative use of the television medium of all time – making today's efforts seem pathetic in their unoriginality – the series has much to teach us about love, sex and romance.

Whilst most pop songs are about either falling in love (e.g. 10cc's 'I'm Not In Love') or being rejected by lovers (most of Bryan Ferry's oeuvre as a single artist, e.g. 'Dance Away The Tears'), few explore the finer subtleties of communication. Leonard Cohen's *Songs of Leonard Cohen* album has some of the most poetic and moving things to say about the travails of romantic love.

4. Authenticity in our careers

New Grub Street by George Gissing remains the definitive account of the tension between writing for profit as a journalist and writing to express yourself or to create art. Although written in the late nineteenth century, the need to earn a living and afford a middle-class lifestyle whilst also doing work that you are proud of and care about remains as difficult to reconcile today as it ever was. The same tension between intrinsic and extrinsic goals and motives is to be found in the excellent *This Bleeding City* by Alex Preston (Faber & Faber, 2011). A harrowing account of life in a bank during the 2008 Credit Crunch, its main protagonist is torn apart by the conflict between his desire to do something worthwhile and his ambition to become rich.

My own book *Office Politics: How to thrive in a world of lying, backstabbing and dirty tricks* (Vermilion, 2013) offers ways to sustain authenticity and succeed in your career. In some respects it is a guide to surviving a problem I explored in my book *Affluenza: How to succeed and stay sane* (Vermilion, 2007), which explained why it is so hard to keep your marbles, in a crazy society.

The John le Carré BBC TV drama series (again available on DVD), *Tinker Tailor Soldier Spy*, is not only gripping to watch, it explores how you can be real and true even while working in the deceitful world of espionage.

Always preoccupied with the problem of what is authentic, John Lennon wrote his song 'Working Class Hero' to express his frustration at the unreality he felt as a result of his massive success. It contains the lines 'There's room at the top they are telling you still / But first you must learn how to smile as you kill.'

5. Playfulness and Vivacity in Parenting

Nancy Mitford's novel *Love in a Cold Climate* provides a delightful portrait of the amusing family culture in which she was raised. The playfulness and vivacity transcend the privileged, aristocratic setting, and offer a model to us all.

My book *Love Bombing: Reset Your Child's Emotional Thermostat* (Karnack Books, 2012) offers a very simple method for sparking love, playfulness and vivacity between you and your children between the ages of three and puberty. It can be undertaken to varying degrees of intensity and seems to change the way you relate to the child. You simply tell them that you are going to spend some time exclusively with them (it is usually the mother who does it, but not necessarily), during which they will be completely in control, and during which time you will shower them with love. In the full version, ideally you take the child away from the family home for the weekend, perhaps leaving on Friday night and returning on Sunday. You ask the child to choose a name for this period together ('Mummy Time' or similar). In the run-up to it, the child finds themselves very excited, and during the weekend, perhaps spent at a bed & breakfast facility or, if you can afford it, a hotel, the child is in charge. Within reason you do whatever he or she wants. You also tell the child that you love them, with real passion. The odd thing is how many parents find that the child suddenly becomes a delight to be with. They in turn rediscover why they were so glad when the baby was first born, or why they love their child.

On returning, you try and arrange to spend half an hour every evening with the same rules (often hard to do, I realize, especially if there are other children – back in the zone, so to speak. Many parents report that a Love Bombing weekend, or some variant of it (perhaps as little as an afternoon), produces dramatic shifts towards greater emotional health in both them and their child.

For fuller instructions on how to do this, read *Love Bombing* or contact me via my website, www.selfishcapitalist.com.

A more academic analysis of playfulness is Donald Winnicott's classic, *Playing and Reality* (Routledge, 2005). The three types of mother I described in this chapter – Hugger, Fleximum and Organizer – are explained in detail in my book *How Not To F*** Them Up* (Vermilion, 2011).

Mike Leigh's 1990 film *Life Is Sweet*, like most of his work, is a model of playfulness, this time in a family setting. Although often very funny, it also portrays the struggle of a defiant teenage girl with bulimia. The tensions in the family are exposed, but the underlying affection and solidarity felt by its members is celebrated, crucially lubricated by playful vivacity.

David Bowie's song 'Kooks', on his *Hunky Dory* album, sympathizes with his son about having such eccentric parents. In actual fact, much of the care for Zowie, as the poor boy was named (subsequently changed by him to Duncan), was provided by a nanny. But the song does encourage playfulness and humility in parents in a beguiling fashion.

Conclusion: Meeting the Challenges

Of all the novels I have read, *Resurrection* by Leo Tolstoy offers the most profound account of how to live an emotionally healthy life. A nobleman has an encounter with a prostitute, who is convicted by the courts as a consequence. The nobleman decides to devote his life to helping her, and is appalled to realize the kind of society he lives in. Along the way, he carves out a much more meaningful *raison d'être*.

Erich Fromm's *The Sane Society* (Routledge, 2001) develops his ideas about emotional health for individuals and society, still the nearest thing there is to a map for sane existence, despite having been written nearly sixty years ago.

Jean-Pierre Jeunet's film *Amelie* (2001) is as uplifting and amusing as can be. An innocent young woman accidentally does someone a favour and decides to start secretly making other people's lives happier. Without the film becoming being corny or sentimental, she succeeds. Needless to say, she also finds love . . .

The song 'Heroes' by David Bowie, from the album of that name, remains the most powerful musical evocation of the power of intimate relationships to transcend external adversities. Equally moving and inspiring is Bowie's song 'Rock'n'roll suicide', with which he ended his album *Ziggy Stardust*. Less well-known is his 'Cygnet Committee', from the album *Space Oddity*. It ends with repetition of the request 'I want to live, I want to live.'

Picture Acknowledgements

The author and publisher would like to thank the following for permission to reproduce the images used in this book:

Page 5 Mae Clarke and Kent Douglas in *Waterloo Bridge* © Hulton Archive / Getty Images

Page 9 Man selling elixir © Old Visuals / Photoshot

Page 13 Mia Farrow with Andre Previn and their children © Alfred Eisenstaedt / Time & Life Pictures / Getty Images

Pages 16–17 Silhouette of an oak tree at sunset © Ken Leslie / Getty Images

Page 35 Mother smiling at baby in bassinet © Constance Bannister Corp / Getty Images

Page 51 Roger Federer at Wimbledon 2012 © Clive Rose / Getty Images

Page 57 Football match © Oli Scarff / Getty Images

Page 67 Ignoring the wife © FPG / Getty Images

Pages 72–3 Daily commute © René Mansi / Getty Images

Page 77 Girl dancing ballet © Martin Pohner / Getty Images

Page 85 Girl in market, India © ARUN EV / Getty Images

Page 100 Father and son play-fighting © Nomadic Luxury / Getty Images

Page 105 A mother toque macaque holds her baby © Sean Gallup / Getty Images

Page 112 Firmine Richard and Daniel Auteuil in *Romuald et Juliette* © REX / Moviestore Collection

Pages 124–5 Packhorse Bridge, Watendlath, the Lake District © Tim Graham / Getty Images

Pages 128–9 Man practising Tai Chi © Martin Puddy / Getty Images

Notes

Notes

Notes

Notes

Notes

TOOLS FOR THINKING

A NEW RANGE OF NOTEBOOKS, PENCILS, CARDS & GIFTS FROM THE SCHOOL OF LIFE

Good thinking requires good tools. To complement our classes, books and therapies, THE SCHOOL OF LIFE now offers a range of stationery products and gifts that are both highly useful and stimulating for the eye and mind.

THESCHOOLOFLIFE.COM

TWITTER.COM/THESCHOOLOFLIFE

If you enjoyed this book, we'd encourage you to check out other titles in the series:

Also available:

Other series from THE SCHOOL OF LIFE:

LIFE LESSONS FROM GREAT THINKERS:
BERGSON, BYRON, FREUD, HOBBES, KIERKEGAARD, NIETZSCHE

If you'd like to explore more good ideas for everyday life, THE SCHOOL OF LIFE runs a regular programme of classes, weekends, secular sermons and events in London and other cities around the world.

Browse our shop and visit:

THESCHOOLOFLIFE.COM
TWITTER.COM/THESCHOOLOFLIFE

panmacmillan.com
twitter.com/panmacmillan